T3-CAO-759

Early Articulation Roundup!

Includes Sounds: B, D, F, G, H, K, M, N, NG, P, T, V, W, and Y!

A Rinky Link Book!

Written by Beverly Foster, M.A., CCC-SLP and Stacy Lynn Foster
Illustrated by Marty Schwartz and Bruce Ink

www.superduperinc.com
1-800-277-8737 · Fax 1-800-978-7379

ISBN 978-1-58650-284-3

Dedication

This book is dedicated to my "Super Duper" family

Greg
Stacy
Julie
Allan
Dolores

Thank you for all your patience, understanding and support!

About the Author

Beverly Foster has earned a Masters Degree in Communication Disorders from the University of the Pacific in Stockton, California. In addition, she received her Certificate of Clinical Competence in Speech-Language Pathology from the American Speech-Language-Hearing Association as well as her California State License. Currently, she is employed as a public school speech-language pathologist in the Elk Grove Unified School District. Beverly resides in Elk Grove, California with her two children. Her hobbies include: writing, exercising, dancing, reading, calligraphy, cake decorating, and traveling.

#BK-305 *Articulation Roundup* • ©2003 Super Duper® Publications • www.superduperinc.com • 1-800-277-8737

Introduction

Dear Friends,

I wrote **Articulation Roundup** to help the busy speech-language pathologist set up an articulation program at the auditory discrimination, syllable, word, phrase and sentence level. This book contains over 200 pages of articulation exercises, auditory discrimination pairs, and word, phrase, and sentence illustrations. It also includes ring covers, certificates and fun game ideas.

As a public school speech-language pathologist primarily working with articulation-delayed students, I wanted to create a motivational articulation program that was fun, yet theoretically based. I think I've accomplished this with **Articulation Roundup**. The child-sized and humorous illustrations are guaranteed to maintain the student's interest and the functional exercises and varying levels of difficulty will certainly appeal to the busy speech-language pathologist.

This book incorporates articulation exercises to help the student feel where the sound is made. Additionally, it has auditory discrimination sections to help the student hear his/her target sound. The clinician says one of the paired words and asks the student to point to the said words. Once the student can successfully discriminate between the two words, the clinician moves on to syllable production. **Articulation Roundup** also includes syllables with both long and short vowels. Once the student can produce the sound at the syllable level, he/she can move on to producing words, phrases and finally sentences.

I hope these fun-filled illustrations and ideas make therapy more enjoyable for both the clinician and student. Feel free to reproduce these worksheets as often as needed for classroom use. Please remember that duplication for an entire school district or workshop is not permitted.

Best wishes,

Bev

Table of Contents

Introduction iii

Activities in Articulation Roundup vi

Parent Letter vii

How to Assemble Booklet viii

Target Sounds

B **1–16**

Initial 1–6

Final 7–12

Medial 13–16

D **17–32**

Initial 17–22

Final 23–28

Medial 29–32

F **33–48**

Initial 33–38

Final 39–44

Medial 45–48

G **49–64**

Initial 49–54

Final 55–60

Medial 61–64

H **65–74**

Initial 65–70

Medial . . . .

71–74 . . . .

K **75–90**

Initial 75–80

Final 81–86

Medial 87–90

M **91–106**

Initial 91–96

Final 97–102

Medial 103–106

N **107–122**
Initial 107–112
Final 113–118
Medial 119–122

NG **123–132**
Final 123–128
Medial . . . .
129–132

P **133–148**
Initial 133–138
Final 139–144
Medial 145–148

T **149–164**
Initial 149–154
Final 155–160
Medial 161–164

V **165–180**
Initial 165–170
Final 171–176
Medial 177–180

W **181–190**
Initial 181–186
Medial . . . .
187–190

Y **191–198**
Initial 191–194
Medial 195–198

Resources Section

Target Book Covers 200–201
Awards and Certificates .202–211
Progress Chart 212
Additional Therapy Ideas 213–214

Activities in Articulation Roundup

1. Oral-Motor Exercises/Articulation Practice: At the beginning of each initial and final section there are exercises for teaching or encouraging the appropriate production of the target sound.

2. Auditory Discrimination Pairs: Each initial and final target section also contains an auditory discrimination section to practice listening and identifying the target sound. This is only a listening activity. There are instructions as well as samples located at the beginning of each initial and final target sections.

3. Syllable Practice: The beginning of each initial and final section includes booklet pages for practicing the target sound in syllables with short and long vowels.

4. Word, Phrase, and Sentence Pictures: Each initial, medial, and final section contains pictures for practicing at the word, phrase, or sentence level.

The Speech-Language Pathologist should decide which sounds and activities to target and include these in the booklet. Some activities/pages may not be appropriate for every student.

#BK-305 *Articulation Roundup* • ©2003 Super Duper® Publications • www.superduperinc.com • 1-800-277-8737

Dear _____,

_____ is doing a great job practicing his/her new sound(s), but we need your help. You will be receiving a small booklet of activities and pictured words, phrases, or sentences after each session.

Please try to practice with your child at least ___x/day, for ___ days per week. Please return this book to each speech session since additional pages will be added. To help encourage and motivate your child, it is very important to listen to his/her speech and praise their successful efforts.

Please let me know if you have any questions or concerns. Thank you for your participation!

We are practicing the following in speech class:

___1) oral-motor exercises (The exercises that we are doing are explained in the booklet.)

___2) auditory discrimination pairs (This is a listening activity that involves listening to a pair of words which differ only in one sound, for example, **pat** and **bat**.)

___3) saying the _____ sound(s) in:
   ___syllables
   ___words
   ___phrases
   ___sentences

Sincerely,

_____
Speech-Language Pathologist

How To Assemble The Target Booklet

Materials Needed:

- Paper cutter/scissors
- Duplicating paper (construction paper weight suggested)
- Hole punch
- Crayons or colored markers
- Optional: laminating paper/film
- Rinky Links or Binder Rings

Directions:

1. After duplicating selected target pages, cut the text or pictures apart using the dotted lines as a guide. The child can color the target pictures.

2. Hole punch each picture in the upper left hand corner through the printed circle.

farmer

3. Have child select a front cover design. Child can use crayons or markers to decorate it. Laminate for durability.

4. Repeat hole punch procedure (see step #2) for child's front cover.

5. Attach front cover and target words to a 1″ to 2 $\frac{1}{2}$″ ring. Ring size will depend on the number of target words.

6. Continue to add pages after each therapy session.

#BK-305 *Articulation Roundup* • ©2003 Super Duper® Publications • www.superduperinc.com • 1-800-277-8737

#BK-305 Articulation Roundup · ©2003 Super Duper® Publications · www.superduperinc.com · 1-800-277-8737

Initial B

<u>b</u>ee

This Book Belongs to _____

Exercises to Promote the "B" Sound

1. Put flavored lip balm on the student's lips. Ask the student to rub his/her lips together. Explain that "B" is made with lips together.

2. Read the nursery rhyme *Baa-Baa Black Sheep*. Have the student make a sheep sound "Baa, Baa."

Word Discrimination

bat   **pat**

Help the student hear the difference between the "B" and "P" sounds. Have the child point to each word as you say it.

Practice initial "B" in syllables with long vowels.

> bā (as in bay)
> bē (as in beam)
> bī (as in bite)
> bō (as in boat)
> bū (as in boot)

Have the student say each syllable after you say it.

Practice initial "B" in syllables with short vowels.

> bă (as in bat)
> bĕ (as in bet)
> bĭ (as in bit)
> bŏ (as in bottle)
> bŭ (as in bun)

Have the student say each syllable after you say it.

Sound Level

I'm practicing my final "B" sound in:

___ **syllables**
___ **words**
___ **phrases**
___ **sentences**

Helper's Log

Sun.	Mon.	Tues.	Wed.	Thurs.	Fri.	Sat.

Please initial the days that you helped _____ say the final "B" sound.

1A

b̲at

2A

b̲it

1B

p̲at

2B

p̲it

3A

b̲ass

4A

b̲ack

3B

p̲ass

4B

p̲ack

#BK-305 Articulation Roundup · ©2003 Super Duper® Publications · www.superduperinc.com · 1-800-277-8737

Initial B Discrimination Page 2

#BK-305 Articulation Roundup · ©2003 Super Duper® Publications · www.superduperinc.com · 1-800-277-8737

bow

back

book

bite

bat

bye

boat

bee

button

bacon

bucket

bottle

bunny

banana

bedtime

belly

#BK-305 Articulation Roundup • ©2003 Super Duper® Publications • www.superduperinc.com • 1-800-277-8737

#BK-305 Articulation Roundup • ©2003 Super Duper® Publications • www.superduperinc.com • 1-800-277-8737

a **b**ig **b**ow

a **b**each **b**ook

buzzing **b**ee

a **b**ug **b**ite

a **b**ig **b**ike

baked **b**eans

ball and **b**at

buy a **b**oat

The boy bakes buns.

The big bug is on a bus.

#BK-305 Articulation Roundup • ©2003 Super Duper® Publications • www.superduperinc.com • 1-800-277-8737

**The bunny bounces
by the bush.**

The monkey bites a banana.

**The boy has a bat
in his backpack.**

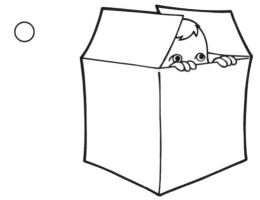

The baby hides in a big box.

**The hippo bounced
on a ball.**

**The band marched
by the bay.**

Final B

ca_b_

This Book Belongs to _____

#BK-305 Articulation Roundup · ©2003 Super Duper® Publications · www.superduperinc.com · 1-800-277-8737

Exercises to Promote the "B" Sound

1. If the student can produce the final "B" in words, have him/her recite the nursery rhyme *Rub-A-Dub-Dub*.

2. Place flavored chapstick on the student's lips. Have him/her put lips together and hold for 5 seconds. Repeat 5 times.

Word Discrimination

cub   *cup*

Help the student hear the difference between the "B" and "P" sounds. Have the child point to each word as you say it.

Practice final "B" in syllables with long vowels.

āb (as in Abe)
ēb (as in "meeb")
īb (as in tribe)
ōb (as in robe)
ūb (as in tube)

Have the student say each syllable after you say it.

Practice final "B" in syllables with short vowels.

ăb (as in cab)
ĕb (as in web)
ĭb (as in rib)
ŏb (as in rob)
ŭb (as in rub)

Have the student say each syllable after you say it.

Sound Level

I'm practicing my final "B" sound in:

___ syllables
___ words
___ phrases
___ sentences

Helper's Log

Sun.	Mon.	Tues.	Wed.	Thurs.	Fri.	Sat.

Please initial the days that you helped _____ say the final "B" sound.

1A

ri**b**

2A

ro**b**e

1B

ri**p**

2B

ro**p**e

3A

cu**b**

4A

ca**b**

3B

cu**p**

4B

ca**p**

#BK-305 Articulation Roundup • ©2003 Super Duper® Publications • www.superduperinc.com • 1-800-277-8737

©2003 Super Duper® Publications • www.superduperinc.com • 1-800-277-8737

we**b**

ca**b**

tu**b**

ro**b**e

cu**b**

tu**b**e

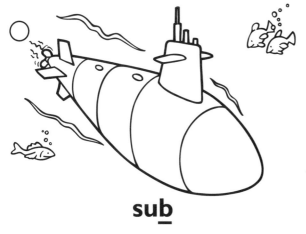

su**b**

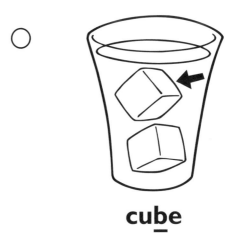

cu**b**e

kno<u>b</u>

cri<u>b</u>

clu<u>b</u>

cra<u>b</u>

glo<u>b</u>e

la<u>b</u>

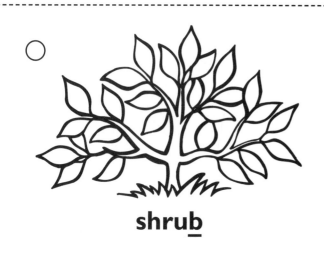

shru<u>b</u>

co<u>b</u>

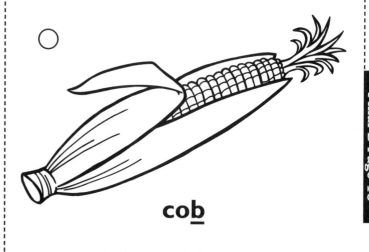

#BK-305 Articulation Roundup • ©2003 Super Duper® Publications • www.superduperinc.com • 1-800-277-8737

#BK-305 Articulation Roundup • ©2003 Super Duper® Publications • www.superduperinc.com • 1-800-277-8737

gra_b_ a ca_b_

a messy bi_b_

a large su_b_

a ro_b_e for De_b_

a spider we_b_ in the tu_b_

a happy cu_b_

sleep in a cri_b_

turn the kno_b_

The cu_b is in the tu_b.

Ga_be wears a ro_be.

#BK-305 Articulation Roundup • ©2003 Super Duper® Publications • www.superduperinc.com • 1-800-277-8737

They ate corn on the co_b.

He scrubs the su_b.

The ant is in the we_b.

Ta_b eats a ri_b.

Can you ru_b my back?

A_be needs a tu_be of toothpaste.

#BK-305 Articulation Roundup • ©2003 Super Duper® Publications • www.superduperinc.com • 1-800-277-8737

ba_b_y

ri_bb_on

peek-a-_b_oo

ca_b_oose

good-_b_ye

cow_b_oy

toy _b_oat

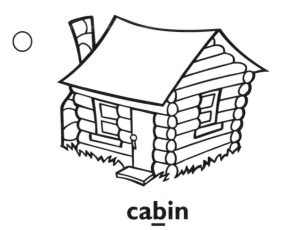

ca_b_in

neigh_bor

ra_bb_it

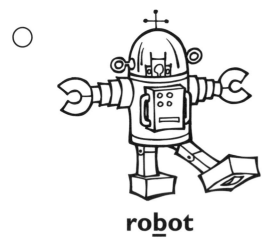

ro_bot

kick_ball

hu_bcap

mail_box

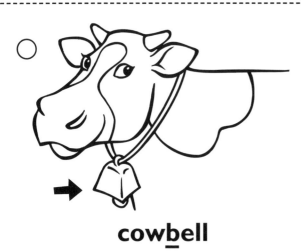

cow_bell

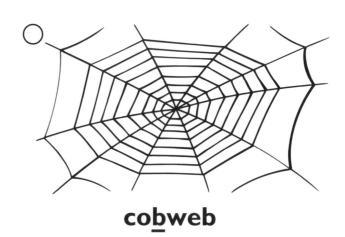

co_bweb

Cut on dotted line

#BK-305 *Articulation Roundup* • ©2003 Super Duper® Publications • www.superduperinc.com • 1-800-277-8737

#BK-305 Articulation Roundup • ©2003 Super Duper® Publications • www.superduperinc.com • 1-800-277-8737

many bu__bb__bles

a big ca__b__oose

good-__b__ye neigh__b__or

a boo-__b__oo

a__b__ove the ta__b__le

ba__b__y bib

two cow__b__oy hats

open the mail__b__ox

He buys bu**bb**legum.

Bo**bb**y blows bu**bb**les.

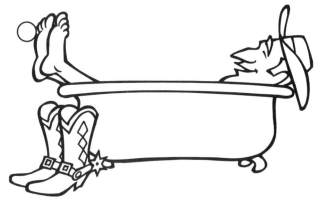

The cow**b**oy is in the tub.

The base**b**all is on the ta**b**le.

The panda eats bam**b**oo.

The ba**b**oon eats meat**b**alls.

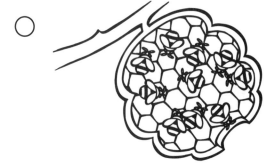

The honey**b**ees are
in the hive.

Bo**bb**y's el**b**ow
has a boo-**b**oo.

#BK-305 *Articulation Roundup* • ©2003 Super Duper® Publications • www.superduperinc.com • 1-800-277-8737

#BK-305 Articulation Roundup • ©2003 Super Duper® Publications • www.superduperinc.com • 1-800-277-8737

Initial D

dog

This Book Belongs to _____

Exercises to Promote the "D" Sound

1. Place a dab of honey or pudding behind the student's top front teeth. Have him/her touch his tongue tip to that spot.

2. Read a *Clifford the Big Red Dog*® story to the student and have him/her practice his/her good "D" sound.

Word Discrimination

dough   **toe**

Help the student hear the difference between the "D" and "T" sounds. Have the child point to each word as you say it.

Practice initial "D" in syllables with long vowels.

dā (as in day)
dē (as in deep)
dī (as in dime)
dō (as in dough)
dū (as in do)

Have the student say each syllable after you say it.

Practice initial "D" in syllables with short vowels.

dă (as in dad)
dĕ (as in den)
dĭ (as in dinner)
dŏ (as in dot)
dŭ (as in duck)

Have the student say each syllable after you say it.

Sound Level

I'm practicing my final "D" sound in:

___ syllables
___ words
___ phrases
___ sentences

Helper's Log

Sun.	Mon.	Tues.	Wed.	Thurs.	Fri.	Sat.

Please initial the days that you helped _____ say the final "D" sound.

door
1A

dough
2A

tore
1B

toe
2B

duck
3A

den
4A

tuck
3B

ten
4B

Cut on dotted line

#BK-305 *Articulation Roundup* • ©2003 Super Duper® Publications • www.superduperinc.com • 1-800-277-8737

day

down

deer

dough

dad

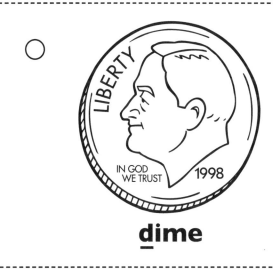

dime

doll

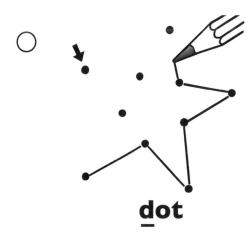

dot

<u>d</u>oughnut

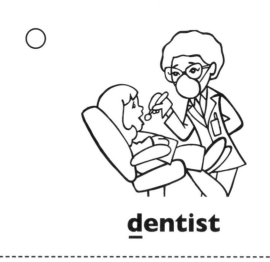

<u>d</u>entist

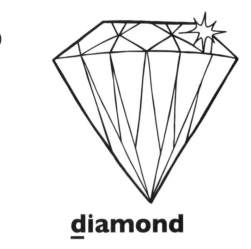

<u>d</u>iamond

<u>d</u>essert

<u>d</u>inosaur

<u>d</u>onkey

<u>d</u>inner

<u>d</u>aughter

#BK-305 *Articulation Roundup* • ©2003 Super Duper® Publications • www.superduperinc.com • 1-800-277-8737

a <u>d</u>ark <u>d</u>ay

<u>D</u>an's <u>d</u>oughnut

www.superduperinc.com • 1-800-277-8737

<u>d</u>igging a <u>d</u>itch

<u>d</u>ots on a <u>d</u>uck

<u>d</u>ancing <u>d</u>ogs

the <u>d</u>en <u>d</u>oor

#BK-305 Articulation Roundup • ©2003 Super Duper® Publications

a <u>d</u>essert for <u>d</u>inner

<u>d</u>oing the <u>d</u>ishes

The <u>d</u>onkey <u>d</u>anced on the <u>d</u>ock.

<u>D</u>aisy has a new <u>d</u>oll.

Cut on dotted line

He <u>d</u>ipped the <u>d</u>oughnut.

<u>D</u>ad's <u>d</u>en is <u>d</u>irty.

#BK-305 *Articulation Roundup* • ©2003 Super Duper® Publications • www.superduperinc.com • 1-800-277-8737

<u>D</u>ebbie <u>d</u>ove in the <u>d</u>eep end.

The <u>d</u>oggie <u>d</u>oor has <u>d</u>ots.

He put a <u>d</u>ime on the <u>d</u>esk.

The <u>d</u>uck likes <u>d</u>oughnuts for <u>d</u>inner.

Final D

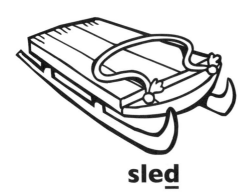

sle_d_

This Book Belongs

to _____

Exercises to Promote the "D" Sound

1. Use a Q-tip® or soft toothbrush to gently touch the area behind the top front teeth. Explain to the student that this is where the tongue is placed.

2. Read *Little Red Riding Hood* and have the student practice a great "D" sound.

Word Discrimination

seed   **seat**

Help the student hear the difference between the "D" and "T" sounds. Have the child point to each word as you say it.

Practice final "D" in syllables with long vowels.

    ād (as in maid)
    ēd (as in feed)
    īd (as in ride)
    ōd (as in toad)
    ūd (as in food)

Have the student say each syllable after you say it.

Practice final "D" in syllables with short vowels.

    ăd (as in add)
    ĕd (as in bed)
    ĭd (as in kid)
    ŏd (as in rod)
    ŭd (as in mud)

Have the student say each syllable after you say it.

Sound Level

I'm practicing my final "D" sound in:

___ **syllables**
___ **words**
___ **phrases**
___ **sentences**

Helper's Log

Sun.	Mon.	Tues.	Wed.	Thurs.	Fri.	Sat.

Please initial the days that you helped
_____ say the final "D" sound.

#BK-305 Articulation Roundup • ©2003 Super Duper® Publications • www.superduperinc.com • 1-800-277-8737

1A **ri<u>d</u>e**

2A **see<u>d</u>**

1B **wri<u>t</u>e**

2B **sea<u>t</u>**

3A **ki<u>d</u>**

4A **fee<u>d</u>**

3B **ki<u>t</u>**

4B **fee<u>t</u>**

#BK-305 Articulation Roundup • ©2003 Super Duper® Publications • www.superduperinc.com • 1-800-277-8737

#BK-305 Articulation Roundup • ©2003 Super Duper® Publications • www.superduperinc.com • 1-800-277-8737

be_d_

woo_d_

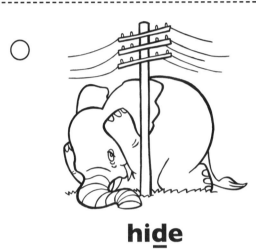

hi_d_e

ma_d_

wee_d_

mu_d_

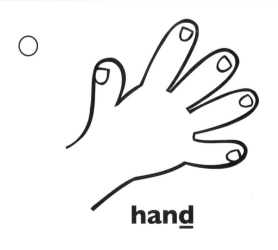

han_d_

toa_d_

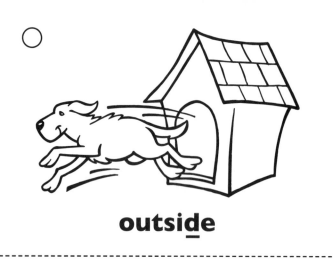

outsid_e_

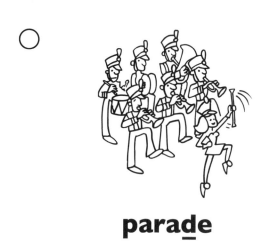

para_d_e

sala_d_

behin_d_

mermai_d_

seawee_d_

besi_d_e

lemona_d_e

#BK-305 Articulation Roundup • ©2003 Super Duper® Publications • www.superduperinc.com • 1-800-277-8737

fin_d_ a toa_d_

hi_d_e an_d_ seek

besi_d_e a sli_d_e

goo_d_ moo_d_

hi_d_e under the be_d_

lou_d_ para_d_e

hea_d_ of the be_d_

insi_d_e an_d_ outsi_d_e

Brad said, "It's time for bed."

He made good food.

The kid played in the band.

I put my hand in the sand.

#BK-305 Articulation Roundup • ©2003 Super Duper® Publications • www.superduperinc.com • 1-800-277-8737

The bride played in the mud.

Did Ned find the toad?

He sawed the wood in the shed.

I fed the lizard.

1-800-277-8737 · www.superduperinc.com · ©2003 Super Duper® Publications · #BK-305 Articulation Roundup

we<u>dd</u>ing

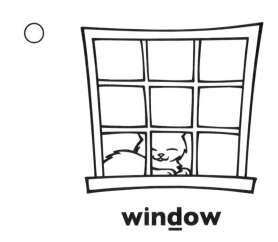

win<u>d</u>ow

bo<u>d</u>y

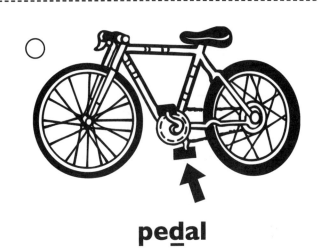

pe<u>d</u>al

fee<u>d</u>ing

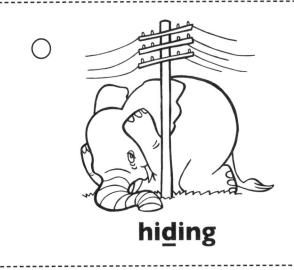

hi<u>d</u>ing

mu<u>dd</u>y

hot <u>d</u>og

sha_d_ow

a_dd_ing

bu_dd_y

mea_d_ow

la_d_y

pu_dd_le

mi_dd_le

pu_dd_ing

Cut on dotted line

#BK-305 Articulation Roundup • ©2003 Super Duper® Publications • www.superduperinc.com • 1-800-277-8737

#BK-305 Articulation Roundup · ©2003 Super Duper® Publications · www.superduperinc.com · 1-800-277-8737

pa<u>dd</u>le the boat

a happy la<u>d</u>y

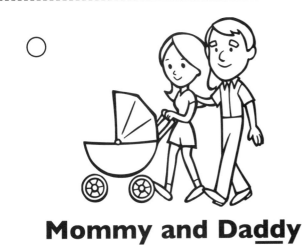

Mommy and Da<u>dd</u>y

eating pu<u>dd</u>ing

fee<u>d</u>ing the baby

mu<u>dd</u>y boots

climb the la<u>dd</u>er

Happy Birth<u>d</u>ay

He is eating a hot **d**og.

She is fee**d**ing the poo**d**le.

She buys can**d**y and so**d**a.

The dog is hi**d**ing.

The la**d**y empties the can**d**y dish.

Da**dd**y opens the win**d**ow.

The duck is in the pu**dd**le.

E**dd**ie won a me**d**al.

Cut on dotted line

#BK-305 Articulation Roundup · ©2003 Super Duper® Publications · www.superduperinc.com · 1-800-277-8737

#BK-305 Articulation Roundup • ©2003 Super Duper® Publications • www.superduperinc.com • 1-800-277-8737

Initial F

_fish

This Book Belongs to _____

Exercises to Promote the "F" Sound

1. Have the student bite on his/her bottom lip and blow. Have the student hold his/her hand in front of his/her mouth to feel the air.

2. Read *Jack and the Beanstalk* to the student. Say "Fee, fie, foe, fum" at the appropriate times in the story.

Word Discrimination

fan   *van*

Help the student hear the difference between the "F" and "V" sounds. Have the child point to each word as you say it.

Practice initial "F" in syllables with long vowels.

fā (as in face)
fē (as in feed)
fī (as in fight)
fō (as in phone)
fū (as in food)

Have the student say each syllable after you say it.

Practice initial "F" in syllables with short vowels.

fă (as in fast)
fĕ (as in feather)
fĭ (as in fit)
fŏ (as in fog)
fŭ (as in fun)

Have the student say each syllable after you say it.

Sound Level

I'm practicing my final "F" sound in:

____ syllables
____ words
____ phrases
____ sentences

Helper's Log

Sun.	Mon.	Tues.	Wed.	Thurs.	Fri.	Sat.

Please initial the days that you helped _____ say the final "F" sound.

1A

fan

2A

face

1B

van

2B

vase

3A

fix

4A

fat

3B

Vic's

4B

vat

#BK-305 *Articulation Roundup* • ©2003 Super Duper® Publications • www.superduperinc.com • 1-800-277-8737

#BK-305 Articulation Roundup • ©2003 Super Duper® Publications • www.superduperinc.com • 1-800-277-8737

<u>f</u>ish

<u>f</u>ire

<u>f</u>ace

<u>f</u>arm

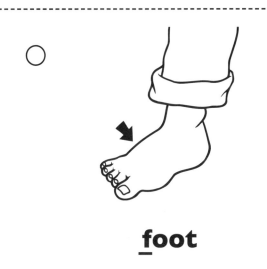

<u>f</u>oot

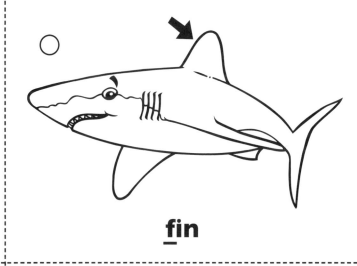

<u>f</u>in

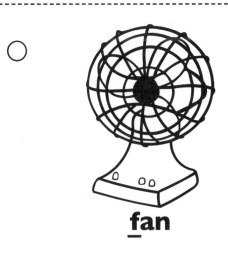

<u>f</u>an

<u>f</u>ood

Cut on dotted line

#BK-305 Articulation Roundup • ©2003 Super Duper® Publications • www.superduperinc.com • 1-800-277-8737

_fountain

_funny

_farmer

_fuzzy

_fireplace

_football

_photo

_family

_family _photo

_funny _face

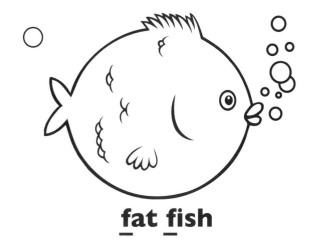

_fat _fish

_fancy _fountain

_fast _fox

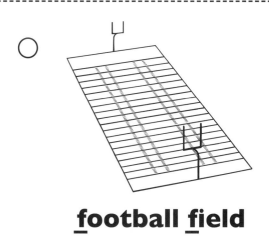

_fix the _fence

_football _field

_five _fast bikes

We _found a _fox.

My _father mows the _field.

**The _fairy _found
a _fancy dress.**

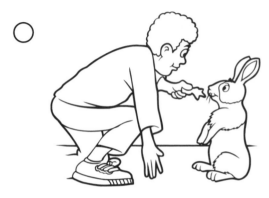

He _feeds the _fuzzy bunny.

She _fixed the _fence.

**_Five _fish swim in
a _fishbowl.**

She makes a _funny _face.

The _family eats _fudge.

Cut on dotted line

#BK-305 Articulation Roundup • ©2003 Super Duper® Publications • www.superduperinc.com • 1-800-277-8737

Initial F Page 38

#BK-305 Articulation Roundup • ©2003 Super Duper® Publications • www.superduperinc.com • 1-800-277-8737

Final F

sa_f_e

This Book Belongs to _____

Exercises to Promote the "F" Sound

1. Apply a dab of flavored lip balm or peanut butter in the center of the student's lower lip. Have the student scrape it off with his/her top front teeth.

2. Read the story *Little Red Riding Hood* to the student. Whenever the word "wolf" appears, pause and have the student say the word "wolf."

Word Discrimination

cuff   cup

Help the student hear the difference between the "F" and "P/V" sounds. Have the child point to each word as you say it.

Practice final "F" in syllables with long vowels.

āf (as in safe)
ēf (as in chief)
īf (as in wife)
ōf (as in loaf)
ūf (as in roof)

Have the student say each syllable after you say it.

Practice final "F" in syllables with short vowels.

ăf (as in half)
ĕf (as in deaf)
ĭf (as in cliff)
ŏf (as in off)
ŭf (as in rough)

Have the student say each syllable after you say it.

Sound Level

I'm practicing my final "F" sound in:

___ **syllables**
___ **words**
___ **phrases**
___ **sentences**

Helper's Log

Sun.	Mon.	Tues.	Wed.	Thurs.	Fri.	Sat.

Please initial the days that you helped _____ say the final "F" sound.

○ 1A

wife

○ 2A

cuff

○ 1B

wipe

○ 2B

cup

○ 3A

leaf

○ 4A

surf

○ 3B

leave

○ 4B

serve

#BK-305 Articulation Roundup • ©2003 Super Duper® Publications • www.superduperinc.com • 1-800-277-8737

o<u>ff</u>

hal<u>f</u>

cou<u>gh</u>

kni<u>f</u>e

el<u>f</u>

wol<u>f</u>

lea<u>f</u>

cal<u>f</u>

photograph

cream puff

handkerchief

blast-off

giraffe

woof-woof

sheriff

show-off

#BK-305 Articulation Roundup • ©2003 Super Duper® Publications • www.superduperinc.com • 1-800-277-8737

huff and puff

Jeff the chef

half a cream puff

safe giraffe

happy chief Cliff

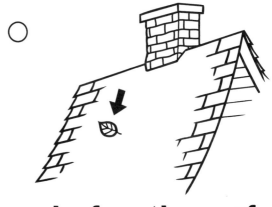

leaf on the roof

an elf on a shelf

tough sheriff

The elf acts rough and tough.

The wolf chased the calf.

Put the knife on the shelf.

She likes to golf by the cliff.

The giraffe eats a leaf off the tree.

The chef cuts the beef in half.

He took a photograph of the kick-off.

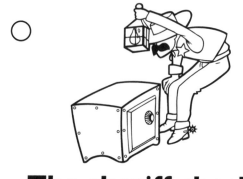

The sheriff checked the safe.

#BK-305 Articulation Roundup • ©2003 Super Duper® Publications • www.superduperinc.com • 1-800-277-8737

#BK-305 Articulation Roundup · ©2003 Super Duper® Publications · www.superduperinc.com · 1-800-277-8737

ta_ff_y

gold_f_ish

laug_h_ing

mu_ff_in

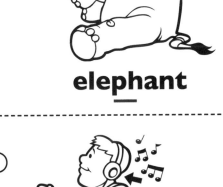

elep_h_ant

gop_h_er

head_ph_ones

dol_ph_in

coffee

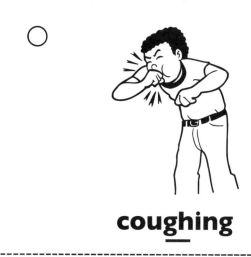

coughing

sofa

waffle

#BK-305 Articulation Roundup • ©2003 Super Duper® Publications • www.superduperinc.com • 1-800-277-8737

buffalo

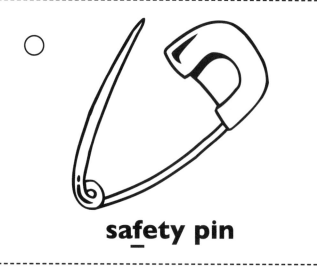

safety pin

ABCDEFGHIJKLMN
OPQRSTUVWXYZ

alphabet

trophy

caught a catfish

alphabet soup

a gopher with headphones

laughing on the phone

#BK-305 Articulation Roundup • ©2003 Super Duper® Publications • www.superduperinc.com • 1-800-277-8737

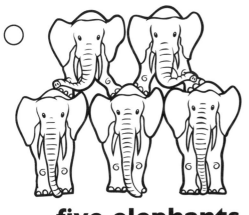

five elephants

a cup of coffee

handful of taffy

breakfast muffin

He has a pocketful of taffy.

The boys are laughing at the elephant.

Count five goldfish in the tank.

The telephone is in the office.

The wolf was huffing and puffing.

The sofa is comfy.

Mom loves muffins and coffee.

They eat waffles for breakfast.

#BK-305 Articulation Roundup • ©2003 Super Duper® Publications • www.superduperinc.com • 1-800-277-8737

#BK-305 Articulation Roundup • ©2003 Super Duper® Publications • www.superduperinc.com • 1-800-277-8737

Initial G

gum

This Book Belongs to _____

Exercises to Promote the "G" Sound

1. Have the student lie on his/her back and tilt his/her head back. This will move the tongue closer to the palate. Now have the student say "G."

2. Using a sugar-free sucker hold the tongue tip down and have the student say a "G" sound.

Word Discrimination

gate   **date**

Help the student hear the difference between the "G" and "D" sounds. Have the child point to each word as you say it.

Practice initial "G" in syllables with long vowels.

gā (as in game)
gē (as in geese)
gī (as in guy)
gō (as in go)
gū (as in goose)

Have the student say each syllable after you say it.

Practice initial "G" in syllables with short vowels.

gă (as in gap)
gĕ (as in get)
gĭ (as in give)
gŏ (as in got)
gŭ (as in gun)

Have the student say each syllable after you say it.

Sound Level

I'm practicing my final "G" sound in:

___ syllables
___ words
___ phrases
___ sentences

Helper's Log

Sun.	Mon.	Tues.	Wed.	Thurs.	Fri.	Sat.

Please initial the days that you helped _____ say the final "G" sound.

#BK-305 Articulation Roundup • ©2003 Super Duper® Publications • www.superduperinc.com • 1-800-277-8737

1A

gate

2A

go

1B

APRIL
1
TUESDAY

date

2B

dough

3A

guy

4A

deer

3B

die

4B

gear

go

golf

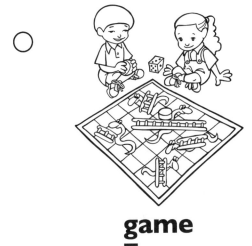

game

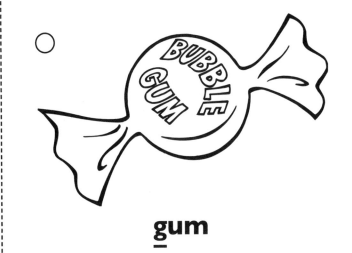

gum

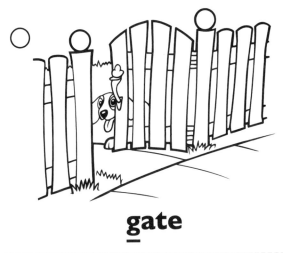

gate

gift

goat

gown

#BK-305 Articulation Roundup • ©2003 Super Duper® Publications • www.superduperinc.com • 1-800-277-8737

good-bye

garden

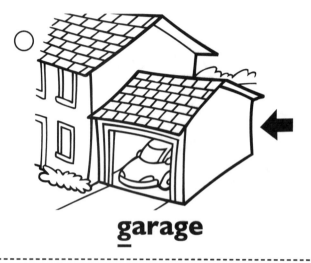

garage

gorilla

garbage

gopher

goldfish

gumdrop

#BK-305 Articulation Roundup • ©2003 Super Duper® Publications • www.superduperinc.com • 1-800-277-8737

#BK-305 Articulation Roundup · ©2003 Super Duper® Publications · www.superduperinc.com · 1-800-277-8737

going to golf

gooey gum

a good gift

gorgeous gown

a gifted goldfish

a goofy gorilla

gobble the gumdrop

in Gary's garden

The guy found a pot of gold.

Gus gave the girl a gift.

Cut on dotted line

The goalie guarded the goal.

The gum is all gone.

#BK-305 Articulation Roundup • ©2003 Super Duper® Publications • www.superduperinc.com • 1-800-277-8737

The go-cart is out of gas.

The funny goose gobbles gumdrops.

The goofy gorilla wore galoshes.

The goat is behind the gate.

#BK-305 Articulation Roundup · ©2003 Super Duper® Publications · www.superduperinc.com · 1-800-277-8737

Final G

pi**g**

This Book Belongs

to _____

Exercises to Promote the "G" Sound

1. Read the *Three Little Pigs*. Have the student practice saying "pig" throughout the story.

2. Look at a book of animals with the student. Have the student point to all the "big" animals and say the word "big."

Word Discrimination

mug   **mud**

Help the student hear the difference between the "G" and "D" sounds. Have the child point to each word as you say it.

Practice final "G" in syllables with long vowels.

āg (as in vague)
ēg (as in league)
īg   (as in tiger)
ōg (as in rogue)
ūg (as in frugal)

Have the student say each syllable after you say it.

Practice final "G" in syllables with short vowels.

ăg (as in bag)
ĕg (as in leg)
ĭg   (as in big)
ŏg (as in fog)
ŭg (as in bug)

Have the student say each syllable after you say it.

Sound Level

I'm practicing my final "G" sound in:

____ **syllables**
____ **words**
____ **phrases**
____ **sentences**

Helper's Log

Sun.	Mon.	Tues.	Wed.	Thurs.	Fri.	Sat.

Please initial the days that you helped _____ say the final "G" sound.

1A

leg

2A

mug

1B

led

2B

mud

#BK-305 Articulation Roundup • ©2003 Super Duper® Publications • www.superduperinc.com • 1-800-277-8737

3A

beg

4A

bug

3B

bed

4B

bud

#BK-305 Articulation Roundup • ©2003 Super Duper® Publications • www.superduperinc.com • 1-800-277-8737

bi<u>g</u>

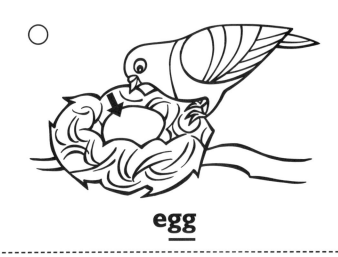

e<u>gg</u>

hu<u>g</u>

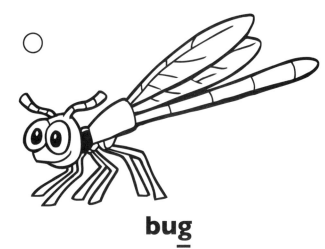

bu<u>g</u>

pi<u>g</u>

ba<u>g</u>

wi<u>g</u>

wa<u>g</u>

handbag

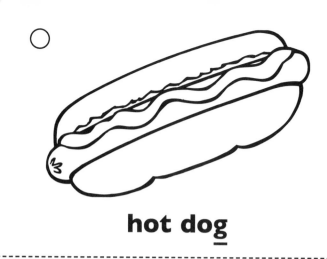

hot dog

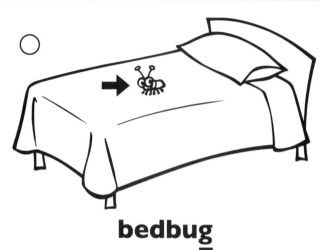

bedbug

bear hug

washrag

ladybug

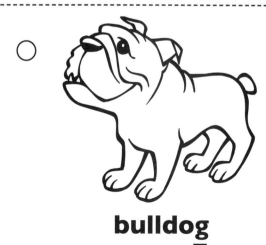

bulldog

bean bag

#BK-305 Articulation Roundup • ©2003 Super Duper® Publications • www.superduperinc.com • 1-800-277-8737

flag in a bag

a big hot dog

1-800-277-8737 • www.superduperinc.com • ©2003 Super Duper® Publications • #BK-305 Articulation Roundup

a dog tag

frog on a log

bug on a rug

a big bear hug

a jog in the fog

a long wig

He put the wi<u>g</u> on the pi<u>g</u>.

She found a do<u>g</u> ta<u>g</u>.

Me<u>g</u> put an e<u>gg</u>
in the mu<u>g</u>.

We caught a bi<u>g</u> ladybu<u>g</u>.

The bu<u>g</u> and the slu<u>g</u>
di<u>d</u> a ji<u>g</u>.

A fro<u>g</u> hopped out
of my handba<u>g</u>.

The lightning bu<u>g</u>
du<u>g</u> a hole.

A bi<u>g</u> pi<u>g</u> is a ho<u>g</u>.

#BK-305 Articulation Roundup • ©2003 Super Duper® Publications • www.superduperinc.com • 1-800-277-8737

#BK-305 Articulation Roundup • ©2003 Super Duper® Publications • www.superduperinc.com • 1-800-277-8737

wagon

giggle

magnet

eagle

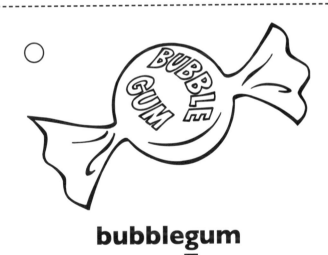

bubblegum

hugging

pigpen

seagull

bea<u>g</u>le

jun<u>g</u>le

jo<u>gg</u>ing

i<u>g</u>loo

#BK-305 *Articulation Roundup* • ©2003 Super Duper® Publications • www.superduperinc.com • 1-800-277-8737

kan<u>g</u>aroo

ju<u>gg</u>ling

dra<u>g</u>on

ti<u>g</u>er

#BK-305 Articulation Roundup · ©2003 Super Duper® Publications · www.superduperinc.com · 1-800-277-8737

digging a hole

a new wagon

a piggy bank

in the doghouse

juggle the balls

a baby buggy

a jogging dragon

a beagle in an igloo

The beagle is in the doghouse.

The kangaroos are hugging.

The seagull puts on goggles.

The tiger lives in the jungle.

The piggy is on a pogo stick.

The eagle is in a wagon.

The doggie is wagging his tail.

He built the biggest igloo.

#BK-305 Articulation Roundup • ©2003 Super Duper® Publications • www.superduperinc.com • 1-800-277-8737

Initial H

<u>h</u>awk

This Book Belongs to _____

#BK-305 Articulation Roundup • ©2003 Super Duper® Publications • www.superduperinc.com • 1-800-277-8737

Exercises to Promote the "H" Sound

1. Pretend to be a panting dog, and say "huh-huh-huh."

2. Go on an "H" hunt. Look around and see how many "H" things you can find.

Word Discrimination

hat   **cat**

Help the student hear the difference between the "H" and "C" sounds. Have the child point to each word as you say it.

Practice initial "H" in syllables with long vowels.

> hā (as in hay)
> hē (as in he)
> hī (as in high)
> hō (as in hose)
> hū (as in hoot)

Have the student say each syllable after you say it.

Practice initial "H" in syllables with short vowels.

> hă (as in hat)
> hĕ (as in head)
> hĭ (as in hit)
> hŏ (as in hot)
> hŭ (as in hut)

Have the student say each syllable after you say it.

Sound Level

I'm practicing my final "H" sound in:

____ syllables
____ words
____ phrases
____ sentences

Helper's Log

Sun.	Mon.	Tues.	Wed.	Thurs.	Fri.	Sat.

Please initial the days that you helped _____ say the final "H" sound.

#BK-305 *Articulation Roundup* • ©2003 Super Duper® Publications • www.superduperinc.com • 1-800-277-8737

1A

hat

2A

he

1B

cat

2B

key

3A

hid

4A

half

3B

kid

4B

calf

#BK-305 Articulation Roundup · ©2003 Super Duper® Publications · www.superduperinc.com · 1-800-277-8737

hot

horse

hop

hat

hair

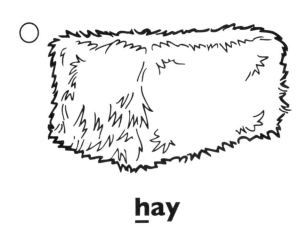

hay

house

hen

hammer

hopscotch

heavy

hockey

happy

handle

honey

hippo

#BK-305 Articulation Roundup • ©2003 Super Duper® Publications • www.superduperinc.com • 1-800-277-8737

#BK-305 Articulation Roundup • ©2003 Super Duper® Publications • www.superduperinc.com • 1-800-277-8737

huge **h**at

happy **h**ippo

heavy **h**andbag

hard **h**elmet

hot **h**amburger

hay for the **h**orse

my **h**ula **h**oop

honk the **h**orn

He feeds <u>h</u>ay to the <u>h</u>orse.

The <u>h</u>eavy <u>h</u>ippo ate a <u>h</u>ot dog.

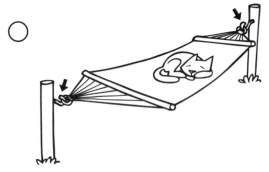

The <u>h</u>ammock <u>h</u>angs on two <u>h</u>ooks.

The <u>h</u>en <u>h</u>as a <u>h</u>elmet on <u>h</u>er <u>h</u>ead.

The <u>h</u>oneybee <u>h</u>urries to the <u>h</u>ive.

We use our <u>h</u>and to wave <u>h</u>ello.

The <u>h</u>appy <u>h</u>amster <u>h</u>ides in the <u>h</u>ouse.

The bunny <u>h</u>ops down the <u>h</u>ill.

#BK-305 Articulation Roundup • ©2003 Super Duper® Publications • www.superduperinc.com • 1-800-277-8737

1-800-277-8737 · www.superduperinc.com · Super Duper® Publications · ©2003 Super Duper® · Articulation Roundup · #BK-305

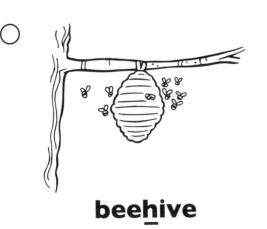

bee<u>h</u>ive

ground<u>h</u>og

hula <u>h</u>oop

dog<u>h</u>ouse

White <u>H</u>ouse

sea <u>h</u>orse

un<u>h</u>appy

be<u>h</u>ind

fire h̲at

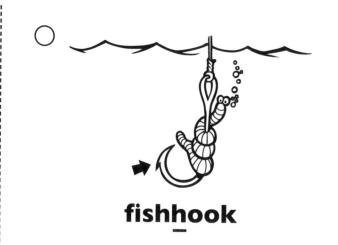

fish̲hook

grass̲hopper

light h̲ouse

foreh̲ead

City H̲all

Oh̲io

rocking h̲orse

#BK-305 Articulation Roundup • ©2003 Super Duper® Publications • www.superduperinc.com • 1-800-277-8737

#BK-305 Articulation Roundup · ©2003 Super Duper® Publications · www.superduperinc.com · 1-800-277-8737

build a doghouse

walk uphill

behind the gate

mom's high heels

bike downhill

paint a dollhouse

ride the rocking horse

a happy grasshopper

The monkey loves his hula _hoop.

The bear finds the bee_hive.

#BK-305 Articulation Roundup • ©2003 Super Duper® Publications • www.superduperinc.com • 1-800-277-8737

The dollhouse is be_hind the bed.

The fish_hook is shiny.

The lighthouse is on the _hill.

Captain Hook yells, "A_hoy, a_hoy."

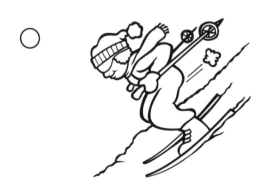

He skis down_hill.

She hides in the dog_house.

#BK-305 Articulation Roundup • ©2003 Super Duper® Publications • www.superduperinc.com • 1-800-277-8737

○ # *Initial K*

<u>k</u>ing

○

This Book Belongs to _____

○ ## *Exercises to Promote the "K" Sound*

1. Have the student pretend to cough making the kuh...kuh... sound.

2. Have the student lie on his/her back and tilt his/her head back. This will move the tongue closer to the palate. Now have the student say "K."

○ ## *Word Discrimination*

key   **tea**

Help the student hear the difference between the "K" and "T" sounds. Have the child point to each word as you say it.

○ ***Practice*** initial "K" in syllables with long vowels.

kā (as in cake)
kē (as in key)
kī (as in kite)
kō (as in coat)
kū (as in coop)

Have the student say each syllable after you say it.

○ ***Practice*** initial "K" in syllables with short vowels.

kă (as in cat)
kĕ (as in kettle)
kĭ (as in kick)
kŏ (as in cob)
kŭ (as in cup)

Have the student say each syllable after you say it.

○ ## *Sound Level*

I'm practicing my final "K" sound in:

____ **syllables**
____ **words**
____ **phrases**
____ **sentences**

○ ## *Helper's Log*

Sun.	Mon.	Tues.	Wed.	Thurs.	Fri.	Sat.

Please initial the days that you helped _____ say the final "K" sound.

○ **1A**

key

○ **2A**

cap

○ **1B**

tea

○ **2B**

tap

#BK-305 Articulation Roundup • ©2003 Super Duper® Publications • www.superduperinc.com • 1-800-277-8737

○ **3A**

call

○ **4A**

cub

○ **3B**

tall

○ **4B**

tub

#BK-305 Articulation Roundup • ©2003 Super Duper® Publications • www.superduperinc.com • 1-800-277-8737

○

<u>c</u>ow

○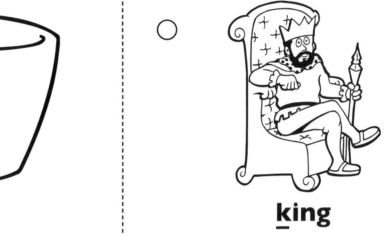

<u>k</u>ey

○ **<u>c</u>up**

○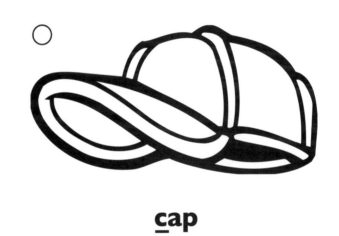

<u>k</u>ing

○

<u>c</u>ar

○ **<u>c</u>ap**

○

<u>c</u>oat

○

Tomatoes

<u>c</u>an

#BK-305 Articulation Roundup • ©2003 Super Duper® Publications • www.superduperinc.com • 1-800-277-8737

<u>c</u>anoe

<u>c</u>andle

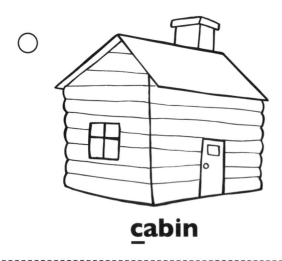

<u>c</u>abin

<u>c</u>owboy

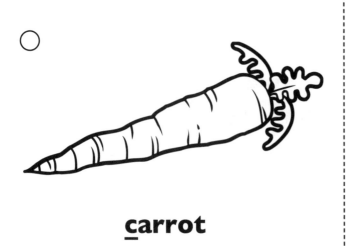

<u>c</u>arrot

<u>c</u>offee

<u>c</u>andy

<u>c</u>amel

#BK-305 Articulation Roundup • ©2003 Super Duper® Publications • www.superduperinc.com • 1-800-277-8737

count the carrots

a coffee cup

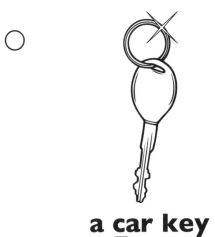

a car key

a candy cane

the cow's coat

a cold cola

the cat's cap

king on a camel

She opens the <u>c</u>an of <u>c</u>arrots.

He eats <u>c</u>orn on the <u>c</u>ob.

She <u>c</u>uts her <u>c</u>urly hair.

He puts on a <u>c</u>owboy <u>c</u>ostume.

She buys <u>c</u>otton <u>c</u>andy.

He has a <u>c</u>up of <u>c</u>offee.

The <u>c</u>ub is in the <u>c</u>ave.

The <u>k</u>ing <u>k</u>isses the <u>k</u>ids.

#BK-305 Articulation Roundup • ©2003 Super Duper® Publications • www.superduperinc.com • 1-800-277-8737

Initial K Page 80

Cut on dotted line

#BK-305 Articulation Roundup • ©2003 Super Duper® Publications • www.superduperinc.com • 1-800-277-8737

Final K

du**ck**

This Book Belongs to _____

Exercises to Promote the "K" Sound

1. Have the student look in a mirror. Use a tongue depressor to gently hold the tongue tip behind the lower teeth. Ask the student to try the "K" sound by lifting the back of the tongue.

2. Read the nursery rhyme *Jack Be Nimble*. Have the student identify and say all the final "K" words.

Word Discrimination

back   **bat**

Help the student hear the difference between the "K" and "T" sounds. Have the child point to each word as you say it.

Practice final "K" in syllables with long vowels.

 āk (as in aches)
ēk (as in beak)
īk (as in like)
ōk (as in oak)
ūk (as in duke)

Have the student say each syllable after you say it.

Practice final "K" in syllables with short vowels.

ăk (as in back)
ĕk (as in neck)
ĭk (as in pick)
ŏk (as in lock)
ŭk (as in luck)

Have the student say each syllable after you say it.

Sound Level

I'm practicing my final "K" sound in:

____ syllables
____ words
____ phrases
____ sentences

Helper's Log

Sun.	Mon.	Tues.	Wed.	Thurs.	Fri.	Sat.

Please initial the days that you helped _____ say the final "K" sound.

1A

ba**c_k**

2A

ne**c_k**

1B

ba**t_**

2B

ne**t_**

#BK-305 *Articulation Roundup* • ©2003 Super Duper® Publications • www.superduperinc.com • 1-800-277-8737

3A

SUNDAY	MONDAY	TUESDAY	WEDNESDAY	THURSDAY	FRIDAY	SATURDAY
1	2	3	4	5	6	7

wee**k_**

4A

POTATOES

sa**c_k**

3B

whea**t_**

4B

sa**t_**

hike

sock

back

neck

week

book

bike

pick

#BK-305 Articulation Roundup • ©2003 Super Duper® Publications • www.superduperinc.com • 1-800-277-8737

drumstick

handshake

music

sidewalk

awake

hammock

snowflake

lipstick

Cut on dotted line

#BK-305 Articulation Roundup • ©2003 Super Duper® Publications • www.superduperinc.com • 1-800-277-8737

#BK-305 Articulation Roundup • ©2003 Super Duper® Publications • www.superduperinc.com • 1-800-277-8737

ta_k_e a pee_k_

a si_ck_ chi_ck_

ba_k_e a ca_k_e

a musi_c_ boo_k_

fantasti_c_ lipsti_ck_

wal_k_ the bi_k_e

li_k_e to hi_k_e

picni_c_ by the la_k_e

The snake is in the sock.

"Tick-Tock" goes the clock.

Let's talk to the cook.

We like to hike.

Quack! Quack!

The duck loves to quack.

Peanut Butter   Grape Jelly

Mom will make a snack.

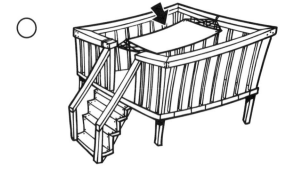

We put a hammock on the deck.

The hawk has a beak.

#BK-305 Articulation Roundup • ©2003 Super Duper® Publications • www.superduperinc.com • 1-800-277-8737

chi_c_ken

pump_k_in

ba_c_on

ho_ck_ey

se_c_ond

ta_c_o

va_c_uum

bu_ck_et

#BK-305 Articulation Roundup · ©2003 Super Duper® Publications · www.superduperinc.com · 1-800-277-8737

#BK-305 *Articulation Roundup* • ©2003 Super Duper® Publications • www.superduperinc.com • 1-800-277-8737

mon**k**ey

kno**c**king

na**pk**in

ja**ck**et

cra**ck**er

po**ck**et

a**c**orn

so**cc**er

ba<u>c</u>on and eggs

a new ja<u>ck</u>et

eat a ta<u>c</u>o

bu<u>ck</u>et of chi<u>ck</u>en

ba<u>k</u>ing coo<u>k</u>ies

my ja<u>ck</u>et po<u>ck</u>et

a so<u>cc</u>er ball

a chi<u>ck</u>en and mon<u>k</u>ey

#BK-305 Articulation Roundup · ©2003 Super Duper® Publications · www.superduperinc.com · 1-800-277-8737

The mon_key is playing ho_c_key.

The kangaroo is ki_c_king the so_cc_er ball.

Mom is ma_king ta_c_os.

He eats pan_ca_kes and ba_c_on.

He hides coo_kies in his po_c_ket.

The chi_c_ken li_kes cra_c_kers.

She is ba_king a cho_c_olate cake.

The chi_c_ken drove a go-_c_art.

#BK-305 Articulation Roundup • ©2003 Super Duper® Publications • www.superduperinc.com • 1-800-277-8737

Initial M

<u>m</u>onkey

This Book Belongs to _____

#BK-305 Articulation Roundup • ©2003 Super Duper® Publications • www.superduperinc.com • 1-800-277-8737

Exercises to Promote the "M" Sound

1. Practice humming different melodies using the "M" sound.

2. Have the student place flavored lip balm on his/her lips. Have the student rub his/her lips together and say, "mmm."

Word Discrimination

mail　　　　*nail*

Help the student hear the difference between the "M" and "N" sounds. Have the child point to each word as you say it.

Practice initial "M" in syllables with long vowels.

mā (as in may)
mē (as in me)
mī (as in my)
mō (as in mole)
mū (as in moo)

Have the student say each syllable after you say it.

Practice initial "M" in syllables with short vowels.

mă (as in mat)
mĕ (as in met)
mĭ (as in mitt)
mŏ (as in mop)
mŭ (as in mutt)

Have the student say each syllable after you say it.

Sound Level

I'm practicing my final "M" sound in:

___ syllables
___ words
___ phrases
___ sentences

Helper's Log

Sun.	Mon.	Tues.	Wed.	Thurs.	Fri.	Sat.

Please initial the days that you helped _____ say the final "M" sound.

#BK-305 *Articulation Roundup* • ©2003 Super Duper® Publications • www.superduperinc.com • 1-800-277-8737

1A

<u>m</u>e

2A

<u>m</u>ap

1B

<u>kn</u>ee

2B

<u>n</u>ap

3A

<u>m</u>eal

4A

<u>m</u>ail

3B

<u>kn</u>eel

4B

<u>n</u>ail

©2003 Super Duper® Publications · www.superduperinc.com · 1-800-277-8737

mud

mat

mow

mad

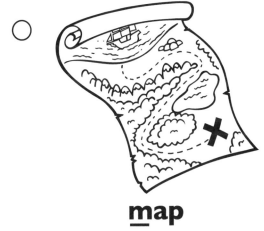

mouth

map

moose

mop

#BK-305 *Articulation Roundup* • ©2003 Super Duper® Publications • www.superduperinc.com • 1-800-277-8737

menu

middle

marble

muffin

money

monkey

magnet

mitten

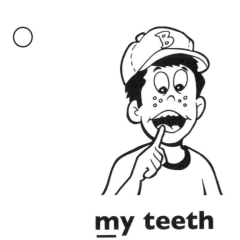

my teeth

man on the moon

making muffins

many monkeys

mouse on a mat

mop up the mud

moose by a mailbox

the major's mustache

He can juggle <u>m</u>any <u>m</u>eatballs.

The <u>m</u>onkeys watch a <u>m</u>ovie.

The <u>m</u>ouse <u>m</u>akes a <u>m</u>ess.

The <u>m</u>an goes to the <u>m</u>all.

<u>M</u>ay I have <u>m</u>ore <u>m</u>ilk?

<u>M</u>y dad <u>m</u>ade <u>m</u>uffins.

She has <u>m</u>atching <u>m</u>ittens.

The <u>m</u>oose <u>m</u>arched up the <u>m</u>ountain.

#BK-305 Articulation Roundup • ©2003 Super Duper® Publications • www.superduperinc.com • 1-800-277-8737

#BK-305 Articulation Roundup • ©2003 Super Duper® Publications • www.superduperinc.com • 1-800-277-8737

Final M

tea**m**

This Book Belongs to _____

Exercises to Promote the "M" Sound

1. Place a tongue depressor or ice cream stick between the student's lips. Have the student hold the tongue depressor for 20 seconds.

2. Place a drop of honey on the student's top lip. Have the student rub his/her lips together. Once the lips come together, practice the "M" sound.

Word Discrimination

comb   cone

Help the student hear the difference between the "M" and "N" sounds. Have the child point to each word as you say it.

Practice final "M" in syllables with long vowels.

ām (as in aim)
ēm (as in dream)
īm (as in dime)
ōm (as in comb)
ūm (as in broom)

Have the student say each syllable after you say it.

Practice final "M" in syllables with short vowels.

ăm (as in ham)
ĕm (as in hem)
ĭm (as in Kim)
ŏm (as in Tom)
ŭm (as in thumb)

Have the student say each syllable after you say it.

Sound Level

I'm practicing my final "M" sound in:

___ syllables
___ words
___ phrases
___ sentences

Helper's Log

Sun.	Mon.	Tues.	Wed.	Thurs.	Fri.	Sat.

Please initial the days that you helped _____ say the final "M" sound.

1A

co<u>mb</u>

2A

LIBERTY

IN GOD
WE TRUST   2003

di<u>me</u>

1B

co<u>n</u>e

2B

di<u>n</u>e

3A

ra<u>m</u>

4A

so<u>me</u>

3B

ra<u>n</u>

4B

su<u>n</u>

#BK-305 *Articulation Roundup* • ©2003 Super Duper® Publications • www.superduperinc.com • 1-800-277-8737

gu_m_

ho_m_e

la_m_b

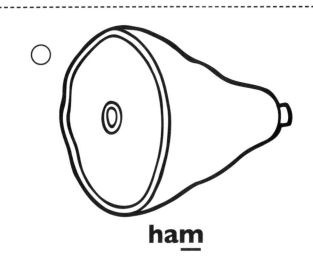

ha_m_

ja_m_

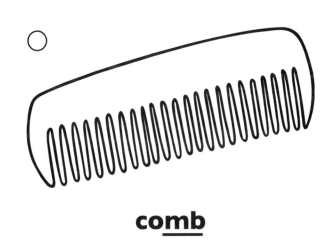

co_m_b

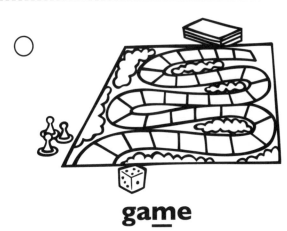

ga_m_e

tea_m_

#BK-305 *Articulation Roundup* • ©2003 Super Duper® Publications • www.superduperinc.com • 1-800-277-8737

bathroo<u>m</u>

blosso<u>m</u>

deni<u>m</u>

ice crea<u>m</u>

botto<u>m</u>

albu<u>m</u>

vacuu<u>m</u>

bedti<u>m</u>e

Cut on dotted line

#BK-305 Articulation Roundup • ©2003 Super Duper® Publications • www.superduperinc.com • 1-800-277-8737

Final M Page 100

#BK-305 Articulation Roundup • ©2003 Super Duper® Publications • www.superduperinc.com • 1-800-277-8737

at the gy_m_

plu_m_ ja_m_

in the bathroo_m_

li_m_e ice crea_m_

botto_m_ li_mb_

a ga_m_e roo_m_

tea_m_ na_m_e

so_m_e bubblegu_m_

He will co_m_b the la_mb_.

He buys so_m_e ja_m_.

Ki_m_ has a pack of gu_m_.

They have the sa_m_e na_m_e.

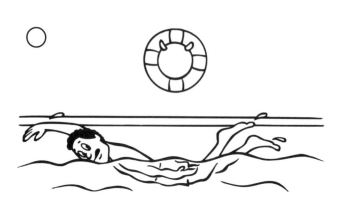

You can swi_m_ at the gy_m_.

The dru_m_ is in the bedroo_m_.

They hu_m_ on the way ho_m_e.

The tea_m_ eats ice crea_m_.

#BK-305 Articulation Roundup • ©2003 Super Duper® Publications • www.superduperinc.com • 1-800-277-8737

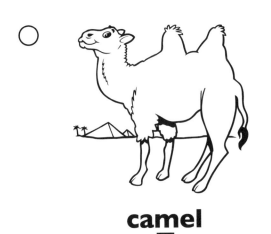

ca_m_el

wo_m_an

www.superduperinc.com • 1-800-277-8737

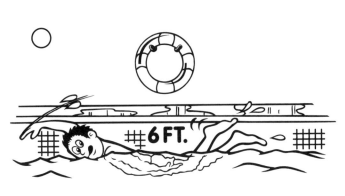

swi_mm_ing

fa_m_ily

#BK-305 *Articulation Roundup* • ©2003 Super Duper® Publications

to_m_ato

fla_m_ingo

ha_mm_ock

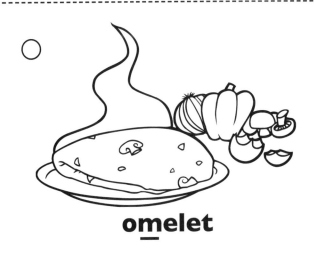

o_m_elet

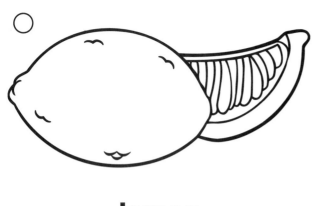

lemon

hammer

climbing

drummer

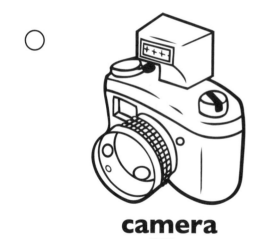

camera

plumber

chimney

domino

#BK-305 Articulation Roundup • ©2003 Super Duper® Publications • www.superduperinc.com • 1-800-277-8737

#BK-305 Articulation Roundup • ©2003 Super Duper® Publications • www.superduperinc.com • 1-800-277-8737

two wo_m_en

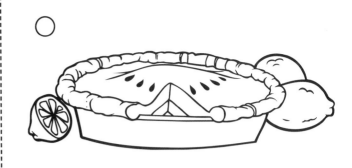

le_m_on pie

a co_m_ic book

lay on a ha_mm_ock

a fa_m_ily picnic

yu_mm_y to_m_ato soup

ha_mm_er and nails

a swi_mm_ing pool

The policeman puts on his helmet.

He is climbing.

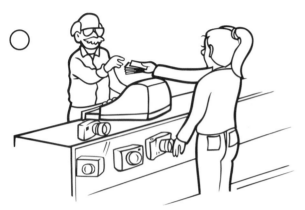

Amy buys a camera.

Pumpkin pie is yummy.

Mom is climbing a mountain.

The family eats fudge.

The woman is on a camel.

Tommy wants tomato soup.

#BK-305 Articulation Roundup • ©2003 Super Duper® Publications • www.superduperinc.com • 1-800-277-8737

#BK-305 Articulation Roundup • ©2003 Super Duper® Publications • www.superduperinc.com • 1-800-277-8737

Initial N

<u>n</u>est

This Book Belongs to _____

Exercises to Promote the "N" Sound

1. Using a gloved hand, place a Cheerio® on the alveolar ridge where the "N" sound is made. The student is instructed to raise his/her tongue tip to the Cheerio®. Have the student hold the Cheerio® for up to five seconds.

2. Have the student place his/her hand on one side of his/her nose and produce "N." He/she should feel it vibrate.

Word Discrimination

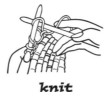

knit   **mitt**

Help the student hear the difference between the "N" and "M" sounds. Have the child point to each word as you say it.

Practice initial "N" in syllables with long vowels.

> nā (as in name)
> nē (as in need)
> nī (as in night)
> nō (as in note)
> nū (as in new)

Have the student say each syllable after you say it.

Practice initial "N" in syllables with short vowels.

> nă (as in nap)
> nĕ (as in net)
> nĭ (as in knit)
> nŏ (as in nod)
> nŭ (as in nut)

Have the student say each syllable after you say it.

Sound Level

I'm practicing my final "N" sound in:

____ syllables
____ words
____ phrases
____ sentences

Helper's Log

Sun.	Mon.	Tues.	Wed.	Thurs.	Fri.	Sat.

Please initial the days that you helped _____ say the final "N" sound.

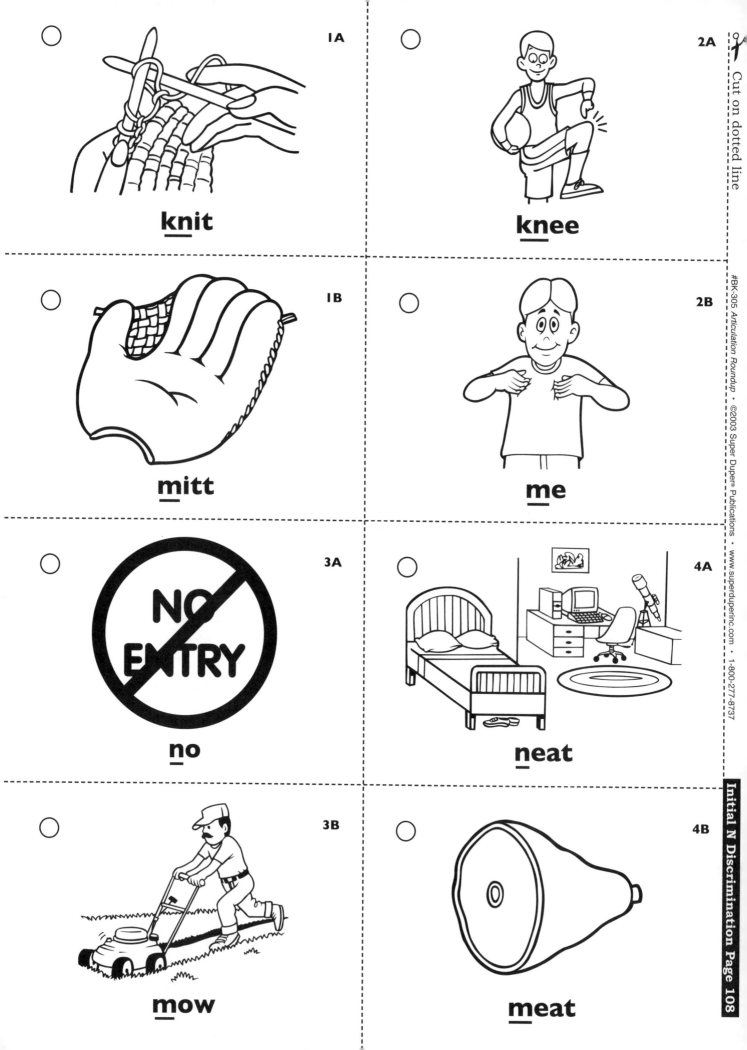

1A
<u>kn</u>it

2A
<u>kn</u>ee

1B
<u>m</u>itt

2B
<u>m</u>e

3A
<u>n</u>o

4A
<u>n</u>eat

3B
<u>m</u>ow

4B
<u>m</u>eat

#BK-305 *Articulation Roundup* • ©2003 Super Duper® Publications • www.superduperinc.com • 1-800-277-8737

#BK-305 *Articulation Roundup* • ©2003 Super Duper® Publications • www.superduperinc.com • 1-800-277-8737

<u>n</u>ew

<u>n</u>ight

<u>kn</u>ee

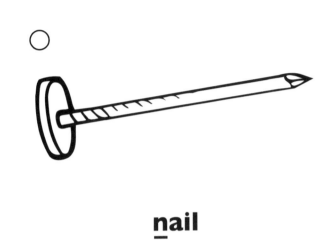

<u>n</u>ail

<u>n</u>ose

<u>n</u>ut

<u>n</u>eck

<u>n</u>et

3

number

Quiet Please
Nursery

nursery

necklace

noodle

#BK-305 Articulation Roundup • ©2003 Super Duper® Publications • www.superduperinc.com • 1-800-277-8737

needle

NEWS
SPELLING BEE
WINNER!

newspaper

LIBERTY 2002
IN GOD WE TRUST

nickel

notebook

#BK-305 Articulation Roundup · ©2003 Super Duper® Publications · www.superduperinc.com · 1-800-277-8737

new nickels

nibble the nuts

noisy nursery

neat nest

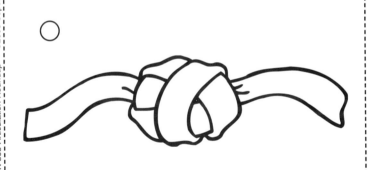

a noodle knot

number in a notebook

nice nurse

a new necklace

The k͟night n͟ibbles the n͟oodles.

She has a n͟ickel n͟ecklace.

Cut on dotted line

The n͟apping goat is n͟oisy.

He n͟eeds a n͟ew n͟otebook.

#BK-305 Articulation Roundup • ©2003 Super Duper® Publications • www.superduperinc.com • 1-800-277-8737

We watch the n͟ews at n͟ight.

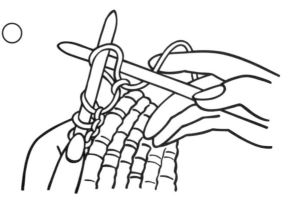

She has k͟nitting n͟eedles.

The n͟urse takes a n͟ap.

We have n͟ew n͟eighbors.

#BK-305 Articulation Roundup • ©2003 Super Duper® Publications • www.superduperinc.com • 1-800-277-8737

Final N

moon

This Book Belongs
to _____

Exercises to Promote the "N" Sound

1. Read the story *Goodnight Moon*. Practice saying a great "N" sound.

2. Using a gloved hand, place a dab of honey or peanut butter just behind the front teeth where the "N" sound is made. Have the student lift his/her tongue up to the honey and leave it.

Word Discrimination

line   **lime**

Help the student hear the difference between the "N" and "M" sounds. Have the child point to each word as you say it.

Practice final "N" in syllables with long vowels.

> ān (as in chain)
> ēn (as in clean)
> īn (as in line)
> ōn (as in own)
> ūn (as in tune)

Have the student say each syllable after you say it.

Practice final "N" in syllables with short vowels.

> ăn (as in pan)
> ĕn (as in hen)
> ĭn (as in win)
> ŏn (as in con)
> ŭn (as in ton)

Have the student say each syllable after you say it.

Sound Level

I'm practicing my final "N" sound in:

___ syllables
___ words
___ phrases
___ sentences

Helper's Log

Sun.	Mon.	Tues.	Wed.	Thurs.	Fri.	Sat.

Please initial the days that you helped _____ say the final "N" sound.

1A

line

2A

phone

1B

lime

2B

foam

#BK-305 Articulation Roundup • ©2003 Super Duper® Publications • www.superduperinc.com • 1-800-277-8737

3A

bean

4A

hen

3B

beam

4B

hem

©2003 Super Duper® Publications • www.superduperinc.com • 1-800-277-8737

#BK-305 Articulation Roundup

o**n**

ca**n**

pa**n**

he**n**

wi**n**

fa**n**

te**n**

gow**n**

Cut on dotted line

#BK-305 Articulation Roundup • ©2003 Super Duper® Publications • www.superduperinc.com • 1-800-277-8737

firema**n**

wago**n**

garde**n**

balloo**n**

butto**n**

cabi**n**

pumpki**n**

chicke**n**

#BK-305 Articulation Roundup • ©2003 Super Duper® Publications • www.superduperinc.com • 1-800-277-8737

i<u>n</u> a wago<u>n</u>

te<u>n</u> me<u>n</u>

ope<u>n</u> a ca<u>n</u>

a clea<u>n</u> va<u>n</u>

o<u>n</u> the moo<u>n</u>

o<u>n</u>e firema<u>n</u>

a mountai<u>n</u> tow<u>n</u>

a fu<u>n</u> lio<u>n</u>

The swan is on the lawn.

The men clean the cabin.

The clown can run.

The chicken has fun in the wagon.

The man is alone on a stone.

The hen holds a balloon.

The woman talks on the phone.

The crown is gone.

#BK-305 Articulation Roundup • ©2003 Super Duper® Publications • www.superduperinc.com • 1-800-277-8737

www.superdupertinc.com · 1-800-277-8737 · ©2003 Super Duper® Publications · #BK-305 Articulation Roundup

pe**nny**

po**n**y

mo**n**ey

bu**nn**y

ba**n**a**n**a

ti**n**y

bo**nn**et

pea**n**ut

honey

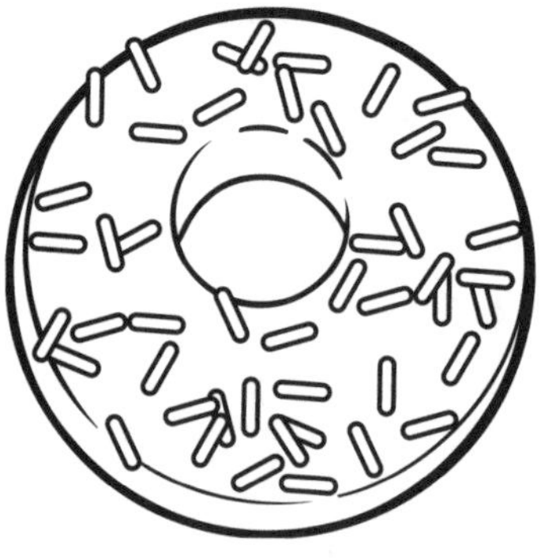

doughnut

opening

canoe

finish

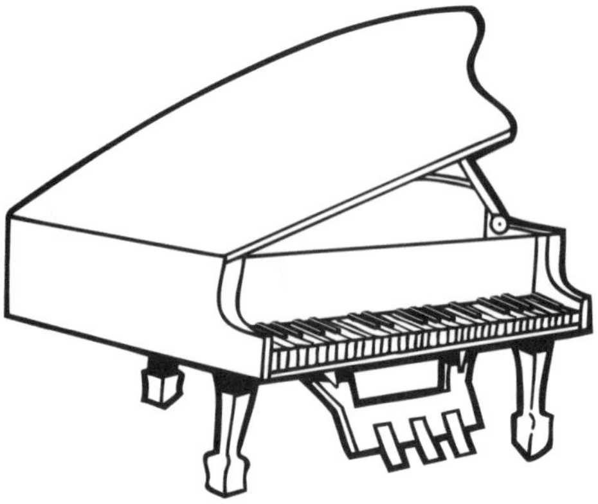

piano

painting

sunny

#BK-305 Articulation Roundup • ©2003 Super Duper® Publications • www.superduperinc.com • 1-800-277-8737

#BK-305 Articulation Roundup • ©2003 Super Duper® Publications • www.superduperinc.com • 1-800-277-8737

a su_nny day

bag of ba_na_nas

a shi_ny pe_nny

a hopping bu_nny

a ti_ny pia_no

a fu_nny pai_nting

a po_ny race

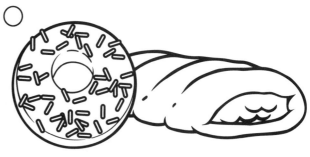

a dough_nut and da_nish

The mo_nkey eats a ba_na_na.

Ma_ny a_nimals live i_n the zoo.

The di_nosaurs play te_nnis.

She pai_nts a ti_ny puppy.

The bu_nnies have a pic_nic.

Da_nny plays the pia_no.

He fou_nd a shi_ny pe_nny.

She cou_nts nine po_nies.

#BK-305 Articulation Roundup • ©2003 Super Duper® Publications • www.superduperinc.com • 1-800-277-8737

#BK-305 Articulation Roundup · ©2003 Super Duper® Publications · www.superduperinc.com · 1-800-277-8737

Final NG

sing

This Book Belongs to _____

Exercises to Promote the "NG" Sound

1. Encourage nasal air flow by having the student hum.

2. Ask the student to close his/her mouth and place a small mirror underneath the nose. Ask him/her to breathe out of his/her nose and try to "steam up" the mirror.

Word Discrimination

sung   **sun**

Help the student hear the difference between the "NG" and "N" sounds. Have the child point to each word as you say it.

Practice final "NG" in syllables with long vowels.

āng (as in sang)
ēng (as in king)
īng (as in mine)
ōng (as in home)
ūng (as in moon)

Have the student say each syllable after you say it.

Practice final "NG" in syllables with short vowels.

ăng (as in man)
ĕng (as in men)
ĭng (as in win)
ŏng (as in long)
ŭng (as in sung)

Have the student say each syllable after you say it.

Sound Level

I'm practicing my final "NG" sound in:

___ syllables
___ words
___ phrases
___ sentences

Helper's Log

Sun.	Mon.	Tues.	Wed.	Thurs.	Fri.	Sat.

Please initial the days that you helped _____ say the final "NG" sound.

cling

long

clean

lawn

tongue

sung

ton

sun

Cut on dotted line

#BK-305 Articulation Roundup • ©2003 Super Duper® Publications • www.superduperinc.com • 1-800-277-8737

wing

long

tongue

king

spring

string

sing

ring

#BK-305 Articulation Roundup • ©2003 Super Duper® Publications • www.superduperinc.com • 1-800-277-8737

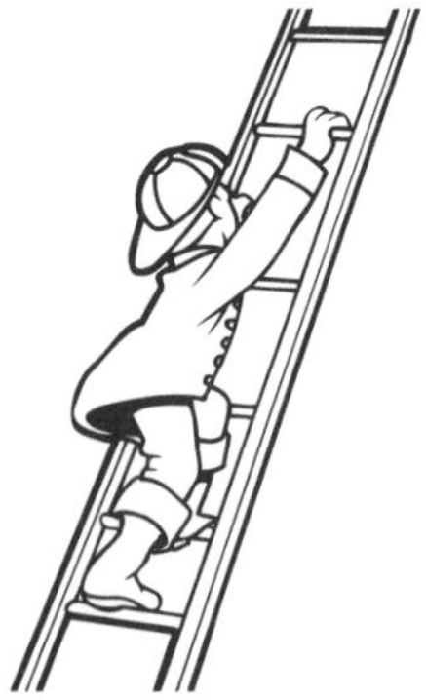

climbing

fishing

jogging

hiding

Ping-Pong

hiking

tying

buying

#BK-305 Articulation Roundup • ©2003 Super Duper® Publications • www.superduperinc.com • 1-800-277-8737

#BK-305 *Articulation Roundup* • ©2003 Super Duper® Publications • www.superduperinc.com • 1-800-277-8737

going home

buying a ring

tying a bow

finishing a song

jogging in spring

climbing and hiding

bring the string

playing Ping Pong

The bells ring in the evening.

He likes to go fishing and jogging.

#BK-305 Articulation Roundup • ©2003 Super Duper® Publications • www.superduperinc.com • 1-800-277-8737

I'm buying flowers in spring.

She loves to go dancing.

The king can sing.

The dog has a long tongue.

The young man is strong.

She is eating pudding.

www.superduperinc.com · 1-800-277-8737

#BK-305 Articulation Roundup · ©2003 Super Duper® Publications

bon<u>g</u>o

jun<u>g</u>le

si<u>ng</u>er

fi<u>ng</u>er

fi<u>ng</u>erpaint

flami<u>ng</u>o

ka<u>ng</u>aroo

fi<u>ng</u>ernail

kin<u>g</u>dom

youn<u>g</u>er

stron<u>g</u>er

mon<u>g</u>oose

marchin<u>g</u> band

Pin<u>g</u> Pong

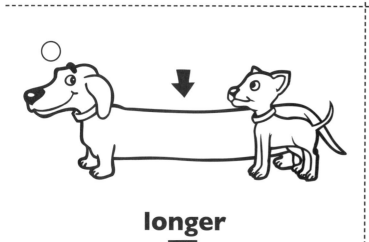

lon<u>g</u>er

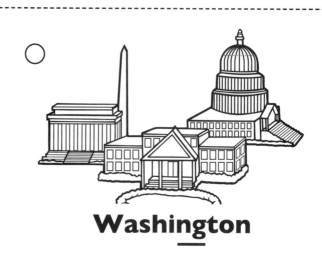

Washin<u>g</u>ton

#BK-305 *Articulation Roundup* • ©2003 Super Duper® Publications • www.superduperinc.com • 1-800-277-8737

#BK-305 Articulation Roundup • ©2003 Super Duper® Publications • www.superduperinc.com • 1-800-277-8737

play the bongo

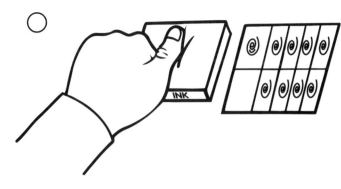

take your fingerprints

a mongoose and a kangaroo

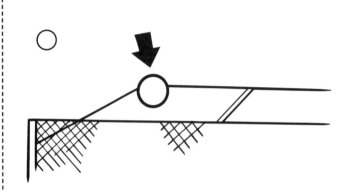

Ping Pong ball

my younger brother

a flamingo in Washington

a jungle kingdom

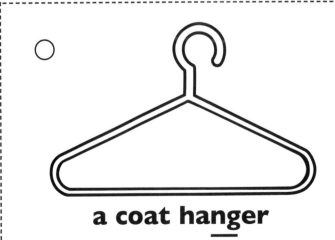

a coat hanger

The mongoose and kangaroo love Ping-Pong.

My younger brother lives in Washington.

Bill is younger and stronger.

The lion is the king of the jungle.

The singer played the bongo.

She is playing in the marching band.

Katie loves chewing gum and flamingos.

Are you coming to Washington?

#BK-305 Articulation Roundup • ©2003 Super Duper® Publications • www.superduperinc.com • 1-800-277-8737

Initial P

pie

www.superduperinc.com · 1-800-277-8737

#BK-305 Articulation Roundup · ©2003 Super Duper® Publications

---

This Book Belongs to _____

Exercises to Promote the "P" Sound

1. Have the student look in a mirror. Tell him/her to rub his/her lips together. Explain that is the place where "P" is made.

2. Present a thin wafer cookie/cracker. Have the student hold the wafer between his/her lips for three seconds. Repeat several times.

Word Discrimination

pear   **bear**

Help the student hear the difference between the "P" and "B" sounds. Have the child point to each word as you say it.

Practice initial "P" in syllables with long vowels.

pā (as in pay)
pē (as in Pete)
pī (as in pie)
pō (as in post)
pū (as in pool)

Have the student say each syllable after you say it.

Practice initial "P" in syllables with short vowels.

pă (as in pat)
pĕ (as in pet)
pĭ (as in pit)
pŏ (as in pot)
pŭ (as in pup)

Have the student say each syllable after you say it.

Sound Level

I'm practicing my final "P" sound in:

____ syllables
____ words
____ phrases
____ sentences

Helper's Log

Sun.	Mon.	Tues.	Wed.	Thurs.	Fri.	Sat.

Please initial the days that you helped _____ say the final "P" sound.

1A

pear

2A

pig

1B

bear

2B

big

3A

peas

4A

push

3B

bees

4B

bush

Cut on dotted line

#BK-305 Articulation Roundup • ©2003 Super Duper® Publications • www.superduperinc.com • 1-800-277-8737

super dup® Publications · www.superduperinc.com · 1-800-277-8737

#BK-305 Articulation Roundup · ©2003 Super Duper® Publications

pie

peas

pin

paint

pot

paw

pack

pig

#BK-305 Articulation Roundup · ©2003 Super Duper® Publications · www.superduperinc.com · 1-800-277-8737

penny

pony

pancake

puddle

panda

picnic

peanut

potato

#BK-305 Articulation Roundup · ©2003 Super Duper® Publications · www.superduperinc.com · 1-800-277-8737

pumpkin pie

pack the pants

pet the pony

pay for pizza

panda in pajamas

a panther's paw

a pig in a pen

paint the puppet

She picks a pansy.

The pig eats a pancake.

He put the pennies in his pocket.

Papa paid for the pizza.

The panda plays in the puddle.

He put a patch on his pants.

She uses a pen and pencil.

He is painting the palace.

#BK-305 Articulation Roundup • ©2003 Super Duper® Publications • www.superduperinc.com • 1-800-277-8737

Final P

ship

This Book Belongs to _____

Exercises to Promote the "P" Sound

1. Read the book *Hop on Pop*. Have the student practice final "P" throughout.

2. Read the book *The Princess and the Pea*. Have the student practice final "P" throughout.

Word Discrimination

cab   **cap**

Help the student hear the difference between the "P" and "B" sounds. Have the child point to each word as you say it.

Practice final "P" in syllables with long vowels.

āp (as in ape)
ēp (as in jeep)
īp (as in ripe)
ōp (as in rope)
ūp (as in troop)

Have the student say each syllable after you say it.

Practice final "P" in syllables with short vowels.

ăp (as in cap)
ĕp (as in step)
ĭp (as in hip)
ŏp (as in hop)
ŭp (as in cup)

Have the student say each syllable after you say it.

Sound Level

I'm practicing my final "P" sound in:

___ syllables
___ words
___ phrases
___ sentences

Helper's Log

Sun.	Mon.	Tues.	Wed.	Thurs.	Fri.	Sat.

Please initial the days that you helped _____ say the final "P" sound.

#BK-305 Articulation Roundup · ©2003 Super Duper® Publications · www.superduperinc.com · 1-800-277-8737

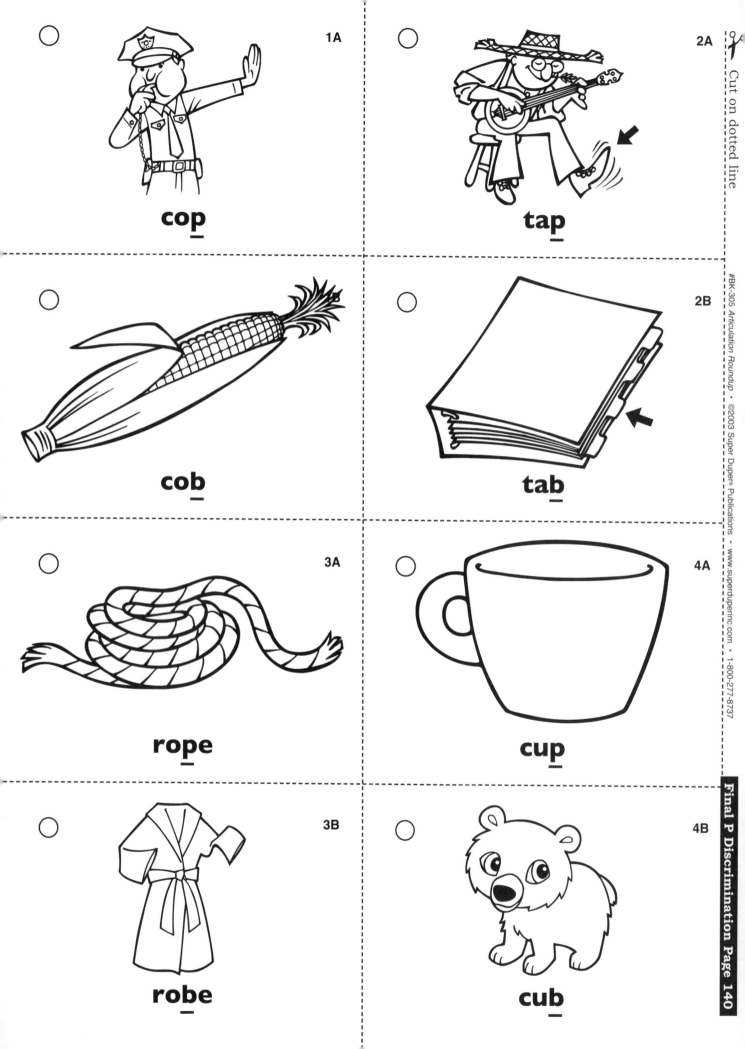

1A

cop

2A

tap

Cut on dotted line

#BK-305 *Articulation Roundup* • ©2003 Super Duper® Publications • www.superduperinc.com • 1-800-277-8737

2B

tab

1B

cob

3A

rope

4A

cup

3B

robe

4B

cub

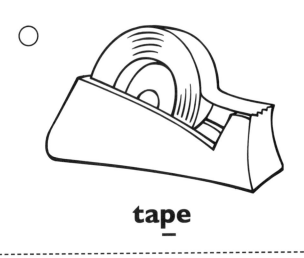

ta_p_e

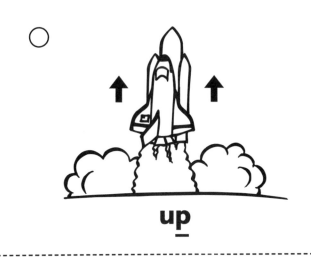

u_p_

ma_p_

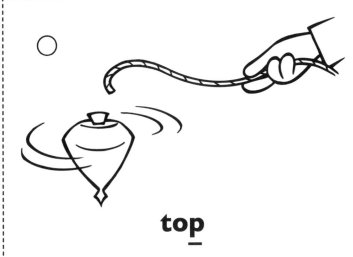

to_p_

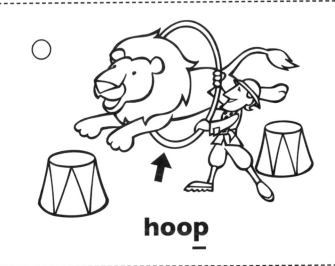

hoo_p_

mo_p_

na_p_

_p_ipe

#BK-305 Articulation Roundup • ©2003 Super Duper® Publications • www.superduperinc.com • 1-800-277-8737

picku̲p

teacu̲p

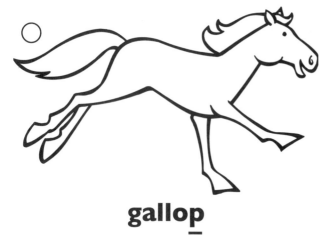

gallo̲p

toy sho̲p

syru̲p

jum̲p rop̲e

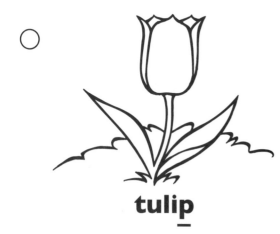

tuli̲p

ketchu̲p

#BK-305 *Articulation Roundup* • ©2003 Super Duper® Publications • www.superduperinc.com • 1-800-277-8737

a cup of syrup

cup of soup

wipe the pipe

top of the hill

hop and skip

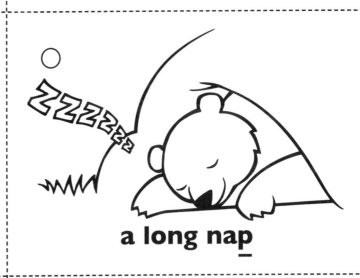

a long nap

some more ketchup

a pup named Skip

He is taking a na**p**.

They mo**p** u**p** the shi**p**.

#BK-305 Articulation Roundup • ©2003 Super Duper® Publications • www.superduperinc.com • 1-800-277-8737

Si**p** tea from a cu**p**.

The horse can gallo**p**.

Can a shee**p**
put on make-u**p**?

We sho**p** for a jum**p** ro**p**e.

Wi**p**e u**p** the ketchu**p**!

The a**p**e can hula hoo**p**.

#BK-305 Articulation Roundup · ©2003 Super Duper® Publications · www.superduperinc.com · 1-800-277-8737

tepee

open

guppy

happy

hippo

puppet

apple pie

mopping

teapot

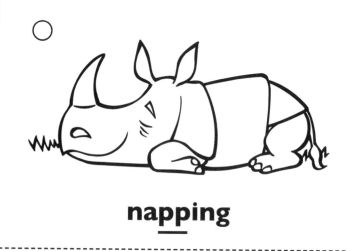

napping

hopping

napkin

chopping

leopard

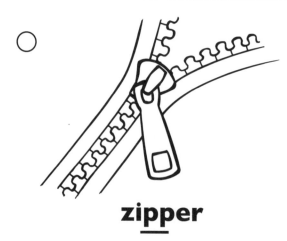

zipper

diaper

#BK-305 Articulation Roundup • ©2003 Super Duper® Publications • www.superduperinc.com • 1-800-277-8737

#BK-305 Articulation Roundup • ©2003 Super Duper® Publications • www.superduperinc.com • 1-800-277-8737

happy hippos

open the package

a napping puppy

bag of apples

tapping a pencil

a hopping bunny

a sleeping leopard

a coat zipper

The hippo eats apple pie.

He pets the puppy.

Mom pops popcorn.

The couple goes shopping.

She is sleeping in a tepee.

She made a pig puppet.

The octopus plays Ping Pong.

The bunny jumped out of the backpack.

Cut on dotted line

#BK-305 Articulation Roundup • ©2003 Super Duper® Publications • www.superduperinc.com • 1-800-277-8737

Medial P Page 148

#BK-305 Articulation Roundup • ©2003 Super Duper® Publications • www.superduperinc.com • 1-800-277-8737

Initial T

10

ten

This Book Belongs

to _____

Exercises to Promote the "T" Sound

1. Place a small dab of pudding or honey behind the top front teeth. Have the student lift his/her tongue to the spot where the sound in produced.

2. Play "magic show" and have the student say, "Ta-da!"

Word Discrimination

tea   **D**

Help the student hear the difference between the "T" and "D" sounds. Have the child point to each word as you say it.

Practice initial "T" in syllables with long vowels.

tā (as in table)
tē (as in team)
tī (as in tie)
tō (as in toe)
tū (as in two)

Have the student say each syllable after you say it.

Practice initial "T" in syllables with short vowels.

tă (as in tab)
tĕ (as in Ted)
tĭ (as in tip)
tŏ (as in tall)
tŭ (as in ton)

Have the student say each syllable after you say it.

Sound Level

I'm practicing my final "T" sound in:

___ syllables
___ words
___ phrases
___ sentences

Helper's Log

Sun.	Mon.	Tues.	Wed.	Thurs.	Fri.	Sat.

Please initial the days that you helped _____ say the final "T" sound.

1A

time

2A

ten

Cut on dotted line

1B

dime

2B

den

#BK-305 Articulation Roundup • ©2003 Super Duper® Publications • www.superduperinc.com • 1-800-277-8737

3A

tear

4A

tea

3B

deer

4B

D

#BK-305 Articulation Roundup · ©2003 Super Duper® Publications · www.superduperinc.com · 1-800-277-8737

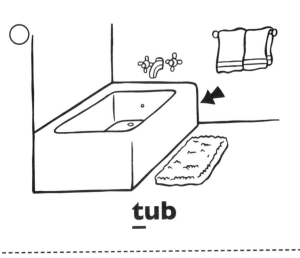

tub

tea

two

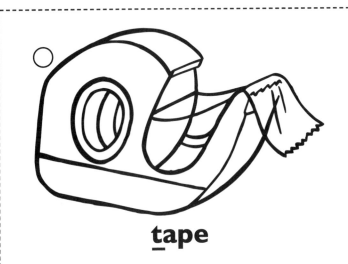

tape

toad

team

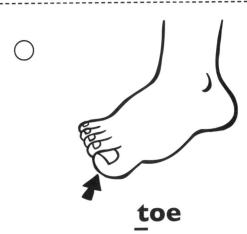

toe

toy

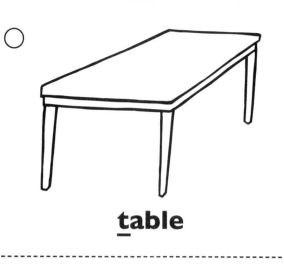

table

tennis

tepee

taxi

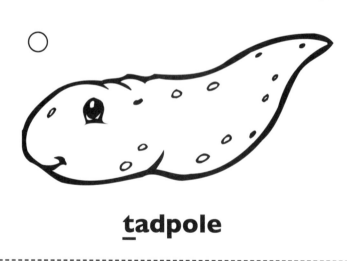

tadpole

tiny

teapot

tapping

#BK-305 Articulation Roundup • ©2003 Super Duper® Publications • www.superduperinc.com • 1-800-277-8737

#BK-305 Articulation Roundup • ©2003 Super Duper® Publications • www.superduperinc.com • 1-800-277-8737

two toads

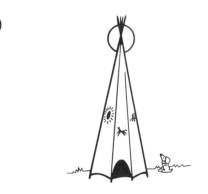

tall tepee

going to town

tap on the table

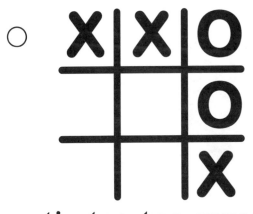

tic-tac-toe game

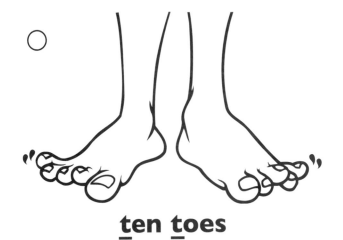

ten toes

toss the tennis ball

taste the taco

Ten tiny toads are in the tank.

He turns on the TV.

They talk to the teacher.

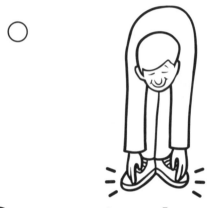

Can you touch your toes?

She holds two teacups.

He takes teddy to bed.

Mom makes tea and toast.

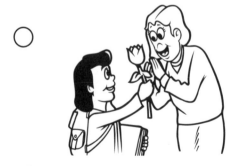

She took the teacher a tulip.

Cut on dotted line

#BK-305 Articulation Roundup • ©2003 Super Duper® Publications • www.superduperinc.com • 1-800-277-8737

Initial T Page 154

#BK-305 Articulation Roundup · ©2003 Super Duper® Publications · www.superduperinc.com · 1-800-277-8737

Final T

bat

This Book Belongs
to _____

Exercises to Promote the "T" Sound

1. Explain to the student that "T" sounds like a clock ticking. Ask the student to make a clock sound "t - t - t - t."

2. Have the student place his/her tongue on the roof of the mouth. Keep the tongue firmly planted on the roof of the mouth. Have the student open and close the jaw.

Word Discrimination

knot   **knock**

Help the student hear the difference between the "T" and "K" sounds. Have the child point to each word as you say it.

Practice final "T" in syllables with long vowels.

āt (as in rate)
ēt (as in eat)
īt (as in bite)
ōt (as in coat)
ūt (as in boot)

Have the student say each syllable after you say it.

Practice final "T" in syllables with short vowels.

ăt (as in cat)
ĕt (as in set)
ĭt (as in sit)
ŏt (as in cot)
ŭt (as in cut)

Have the student say each syllable after you say it.

Sound Level

I'm practicing my final "T" sound in:

____ syllables
____ words
____ phrases
____ sentences

Helper's Log

Sun.	Mon.	Tues.	Wed.	Thurs.	Fri.	Sat.

Please initial the days that you helped _____ say the final "T" sound.

1A si**t**

2A bi**t**e

1B si**ck**

2B bi**k**e

3A kno**t**

4A ba**t**

3B kno**ck**

4B ba**ck**

#BK-305 Articulation Roundup • ©2003 Super Duper® Publications • www.superduperinc.com • 1-800-277-8737

nigh_t

ha_t

©2003 Super Duper® Publications • www.superduperinc.com • 1-800-277-8737

we_t

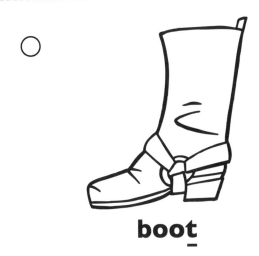

boo_t

whi_te

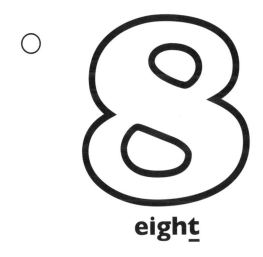

eigh_t

nu_t

ho_t

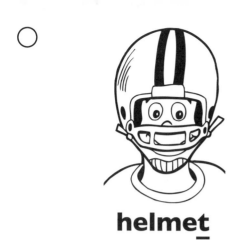

helme_t_

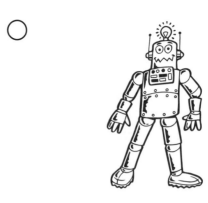

robo_t_

bonne_t_

rabbi_t_

doughnu_t_

walle_t_

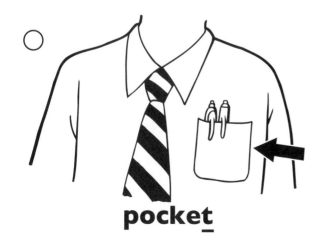

pocke_t_

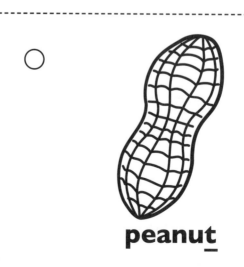

peanu_t_

#BK-305 Articulation Roundup • ©2003 Super Duper® Publications • www.superduperinc.com • 1-800-277-8737

#BK-305 Articulation Roundup • ©2003 Super Duper® Publications • www.superduperinc.com • 1-800-277-8737

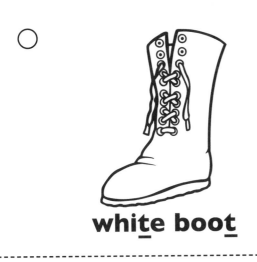

white boot

a fat bat

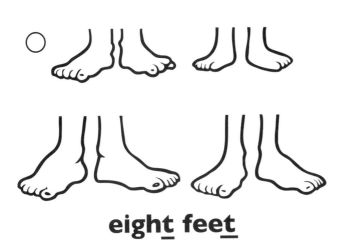

eight feet

late at night

bite a doughnut

bright light

a pet cat

hot plate

We count eight kites.

The knight will eat a doughnut.

He ate late at night.

He has a pet rabbit.

The fat cat chased the rat.

She put on a fuzzy coat.

The white boat can float.

He bought a bat and mitt.

#BK-305 Articulation Roundup • ©2003 Super Duper® Publications • www.superduperinc.com • 1-800-277-8737

#BK-305 Articulation Roundup • ©2003 Super Duper® Publications • www.superduperinc.com • 1-800-277-8737

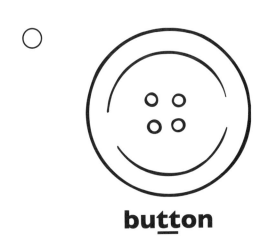

bu_t_ton

ki_t_ten

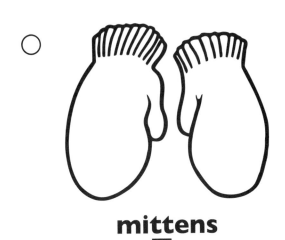

mi_t_tens

ba_t_on

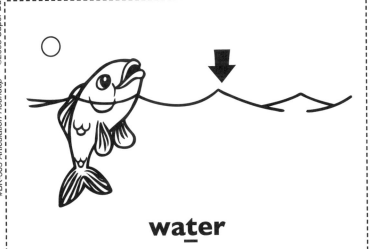

wa_t_er

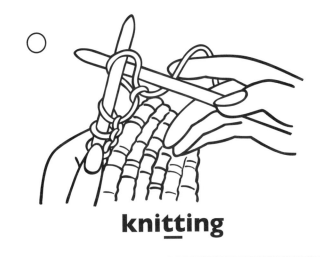

kni_t_ting

ea_t_ing

pho_t_o

cheetah

cotton candy

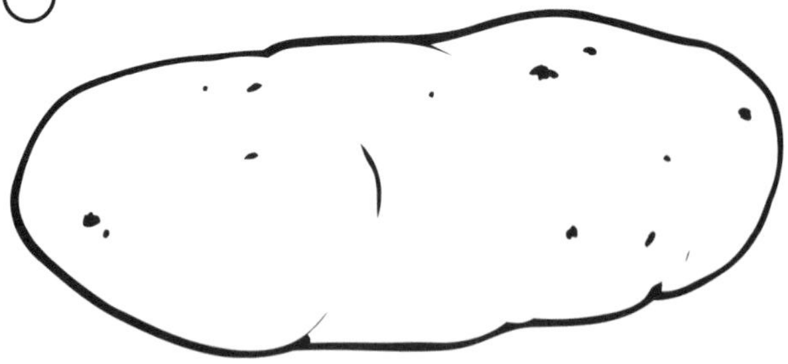

potato

guitar

lettuce

motor

sweater

computer

#BK-305 Articulation Roundup • ©2003 Super Duper® Publications • www.superduperinc.com • 1-800-277-8737

#BK-305 Articulation Roundup · ©2003 Super Duper® Publications · www.superduperinc.com · 1-800-277-8737

a baked po_ta_to

tip_toe to bed

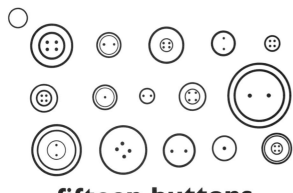

fif_teen but_tons

pe_t_ting a ki_t_ten

ea_t_ing co_t_ton candy

a li_t_tle co_t_tage

a lap_top comp_u_ter

playing gui_t_ar

He is biting in**to** a doughnu**t**.

She is ice ska**t**ing.

#BK-305 Articulation Roundup • ©2003 Super Duper® Publications • www.superduperinc.com • 1-800-277-8737

A po**t**a**t**o is a vege**t**able.

Mom is kni**tt**ing a swea**t**er.

He is ea**t**ing co**tt**on candy.

He takes pho**t**os of the chee**t**ah.

Dad is cu**tt**ing the wa**t**ermelon.

The ki**tt**ens lost their mi**tt**ens.

#BK-305 Articulation Roundup • ©2003 Super Duper® Publications • www.superduperinc.com • 1-800-277-8737

Initial V

<u>v</u>an

This Book Belongs to _____

Exercises to Promote the "V" Sound

1. Have the student gently bite his/her lower lip and blow while turning on his/her voice.

2. Make valentines with the student. Have him/her practice a great "V" sound.

Word Discrimination

vase　　　**base**

Help the student hear the difference between the "V" and "B" sounds. Have the child point to each word as you say it.

Practice initial "V" in syllables with long vowels.

> vā (as in vane)
> vē (as in veto)
> vī (as in vine)
> vō (as in vote)
> vū (as in view)

Have the student say each syllable after you say it.

Practice initial "V" in syllables with short vowels.

> vă (as in vat)
> vĕ (as in vet)
> vĭ (as in visit)
> vŏ (as in vault)
> vŭ (as in vulture)

Have the student say each syllable after you say it.

Sound Level

I'm practicing my final "V" sound in:

___ syllables
___ words
___ phrases
___ sentences

Helper's Log

Sun.	Mon.	Tues.	Wed.	Thurs.	Fri.	Sat.

Please initial the days that you helped _____ say the final "V" sound.

1A

vote

2A

v

1B

boat

2B

bee

3A

vase

4A

vest

3B

base

4B

best

#BK-305 *Articulation Roundup* • ©2003 Super Duper® Publications • www.superduperinc.com • 1-800-277-8737

#BK-305 Articulation Roundup • ©2003 Super Duper® Publications • www.superduperinc.com • 1-800-277-8737

<u>v</u>ine

<u>v</u>an

<u>v</u>ote

<u>v</u>et

<u>v</u>ase

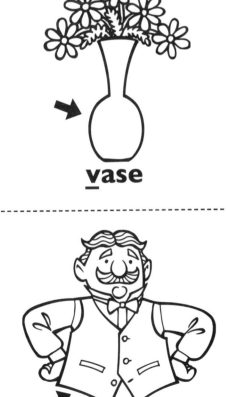

<u>v</u>eil

<u>v</u>est

<u>v</u>oice

valentine

village

volcano

vegetables

vacuum

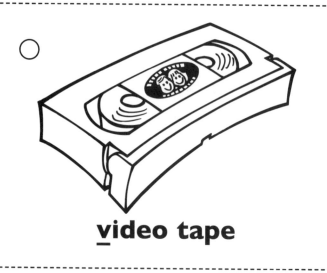

video tape

visit

valley

#BK-305 Articulation Roundup • ©2003 Super Duper® Publications • www.superduperinc.com • 1-800-277-8737

#BK-305 Articulation Roundup · ©2003 Super Duper® Publications · www.superduperinc.com · 1-800-277-8737

a glass <u>v</u>ase

the family <u>v</u>an

a <u>v</u>ampire costume

<u>v</u>alentine cookies

play a <u>v</u>iolin

a basket of <u>v</u>egetables

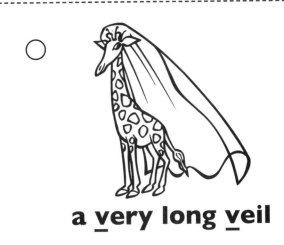

a <u>v</u>ery long <u>v</u>eil

<u>v</u>isit the <u>v</u>et

#BK-305 *Articulation Roundup* • ©2003 Super Duper® Publications • www.superduperinc.com • 1-800-277-8737

The vampire plays the violin.

The bunny eats the vegetables.

Put the violets in the vase.

Dad puts the TV in the van.

She eats vanilla pudding.

He swings on a vine.

The vacuum is very loud.

She buys a video game.

#BK-305 Articulation Roundup • ©2003 Super Duper® Publications • www.superduperinc.com • 1-800-277-8737

Initial V

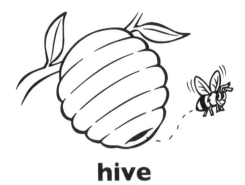

hi**v**e

This Book Belongs
to _____

Exercises to Promote the "V" Sound

1. Put graham cracker cookie crumbs on the student's bottom lip. While looking, have the student scrape it off with his/her front teeth.

2. Have a pretend "wedding" and wear a veil or fill up the "van" with all kinds of things.

Word Discrimination

cave

cape

Help the student hear the difference between the "V" and "P/F" sounds. Have the child point to each word as you say it.

Practice final "V" in syllables with long vowels.

$\bar{a}$v (as in cave)
$\bar{e}$v (as in sleeve)
$\bar{i}$v (as in hive)
$\bar{o}$v (as in stove)
$\bar{u}$v (as in groove)

Have the student say each syllable after you say it.

Practice final "V" in syllables with short vowels.

$\breve{a}$v (as in have)
$\breve{e}$v (as in level)
$\breve{i}$v (as in give)
$\breve{o}$v (as in suave)
$\breve{u}$v (as in glove)

Have the student say each syllable after you say it.

Sound Level

I'm practicing my final "V" sound in:

___ **syllables**
___ **words**
___ **phrases**
___ **sentences**

Helper's Log

Sun.	Mon.	Tues.	Wed.	Thurs.	Fri.	Sat.

Please initial the days that you helped _____ say the final "V" sound.

1A

cave

2A

leave

1B

cape

2B

leaf

3A

save

4A

have

3B

safe

4B

half

#BK-305 Articulation Roundup • ©2003 Super Duper® Publications • www.superduperinc.com • 1-800-277-8737

mo_v_e

ca_v_e

©2003 Super Duper® Publications • www.superduperinc.com • 1-800-277-8737

gi_v_e

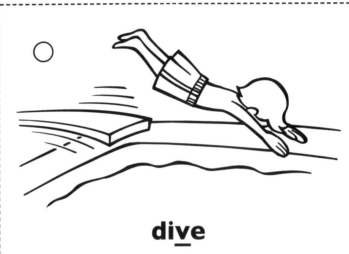

di_v_e

#BK-305 Articulation Roundup •

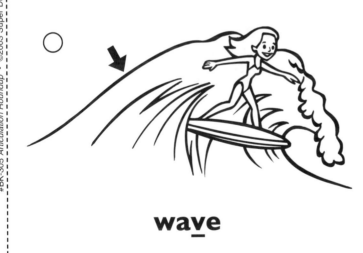

wa_v_e

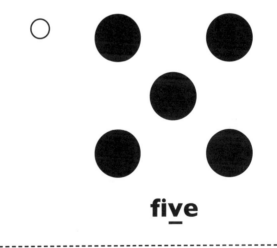

fi_v_e

lo_v_e

sa_v_e

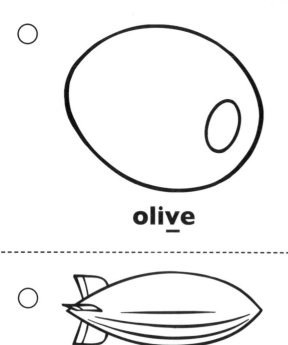

oli_ve_

beehi_ve_

abo_ve_

relati_ve_

sha_ve_

slee_ve_

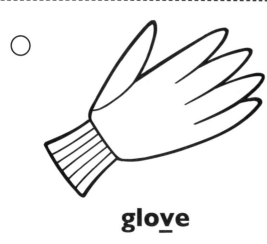

_g_lo_ve_

sto_ve_

#BK-305 Articulation Roundup • ©2003 Super Duper® Publications • www.superduperinc.com • 1-800-277-8737

#BK-305 Articulation Roundup • ©2003 Super Duper® Publications • www.superduperinc.com • 1-800-277-8737

a white do_v_e

gi_v_e a gift

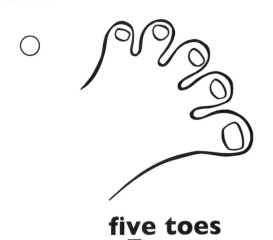

fi_v_e toes

mo_v_e the box

wa_v_e good-bye

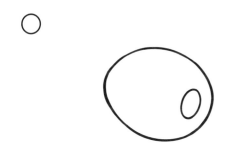

a salty oli_v_e

a bat ca_v_e

abo_v_e the clouds

Bees live in a hive.

The bear will leave the cave.

Dad gave me a glove.

The dove flies above the tree.

Dave is brave.

The stove is very hot.

The wave is big.

They have five dogs.

#BK-305 Articulation Roundup • ©2003 Super Duper® Publications • www.superduperinc.com • 1-800-277-8737

#BK-305 Articulation Roundup • ©2003 Super Duper® Publications • www.superduperinc.com • 1-800-277-8737

sho_vel

ele_ven

mo_vie

la_va

i_vy

sha_ving

o_ven

se_ven

hea_v_y

se_v_enty

bea_v_er

o_v_er

lea_v_ing

clo_v_er

Na_v_y

en_v_elope

#BK-305 Articulation Roundup • ©2003 Super Duper® Publications • www.superduperinc.com • 1-800-277-8737

#BK-305 Articulation Roundup • ©2003 Super Duper® Publications • www.superduperinc.com • 1-800-277-8737

se<u>v</u>en pennies

hea<u>v</u>y package

wa<u>v</u>ing good-bye

watching a mo<u>v</u>ie

di<u>v</u>ing into the pool

mail the en<u>v</u>elope

sho<u>v</u>el the snow

busy bea<u>v</u>er

The kids feed the se_v_en ducks.

The tele_v_ision is hea_v_y.

The toad hops o_v_er the puddle.

The hippos are ha_v_ing fun.

He is sa_v_ing comic books.

The la_v_a came from the volcano.

They are lea_v_ing the beach.

She puts a valentine in the en_v_elope.

#BK-305 Articulation Roundup • ©2003 Super Duper® Publications • www.superduperinc.com • 1-800-277-8737

#BK-305 Articulation Roundup • ©2003 Super Duper® Publications • www.superduperinc.com • 1-800-277-8737

Initial W

<u>w</u>atch

This Book Belongs to _____

Exercises to Promote the "W" Sound

1. Using a mirror, instruct the student to purse his/her lips and then retract them into a smiling position. Repeat 10x.

2. Ask the student to purse his/her lips in the "oo" (as in spoon) position. Next, ask the student to relax his/her lips and say "ah." Continue repeating this pattern so the student will be making "wah-wah-wah" syllables.

Word Discrimination

wake   *lake*

Help the student hear the difference between the "W" and "L/V" sounds. Have the child point to each word as you say it.

Practice initial "W" in syllables with long vowels.

wā (as in wave)
wē (as in weed)
wī (as in white)
wō (as in woke)
wū (as in woo)

Have the student say each syllable after you say it.

Practice initial "W" in syllables with short vowels.

wă (as in wax)
wĕ (as in wet)
wĭ (as in wit)
wŏ (as in watch)
wŭ (as in won)

Have the student say each syllable after you say it.

Sound Level

I'm practicing my final "W" sound in:

___ syllables
___ words
___ phrases
___ sentences

Helper's Log

Sun.	Mon.	Tues.	Wed.	Thurs.	Fri.	Sat.

Please initial the days that you helped _____ say the final "W" sound.

wake

white

lake

light

west

wet

vest

vet

#BK-305 Articulation Roundup • ©2003 Super Duper® Publications • www.superduperinc.com • 1-800-277-8737

#BK-305 Articulation Roundup • ©2003 Super Duper® Publications • www.superduperinc.com • 1-800-277-8737

web

weed

we

wig

one

wood

win

wet

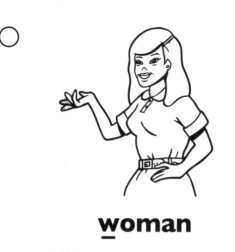

woman

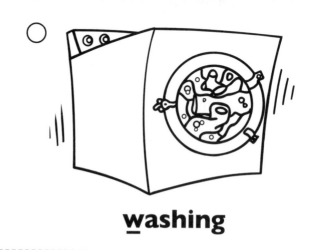

washing

walking

waking

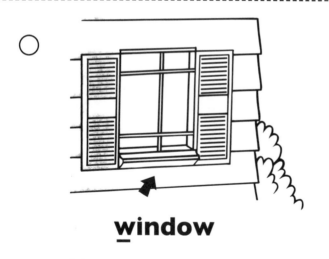

window

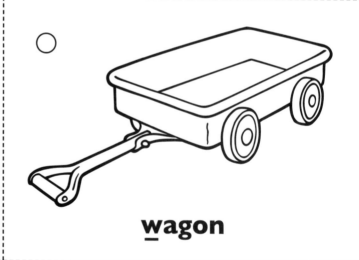

wagon

windy

wedding

#BK-305 *Articulation Roundup* • ©2003 Super Duper® Publications • www.superduperinc.com • 1-800-277-8737

#BK-305 Articulation Roundup · ©2003 Super Duper® Publications · www.superduperinc.com · 1-800-277-8737

1A

walk the dog

2A

wash the **w**indows

1B

a **w**et **w**itch

2B

WINDY LANE

a **w**indy day

3A

wagon **w**heel

4A

wolf in the **w**oods

3B

wave to the **w**oman

4B

one **w**affle

The <u>w</u>olf lives in the <u>w</u>oods.

The <u>w</u>itch buys a <u>w</u>ig.

The dog says, "<u>W</u>oof-woof."

A <u>w</u>oman <u>w</u>ipes the table.

<u>W</u>e like to <u>w</u>ash <u>w</u>indows.

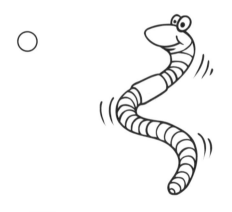

The <u>w</u>orm can <u>w</u>iggle.

He <u>w</u>ants <u>w</u>affles.

They <u>w</u>alk in the <u>w</u>ater.

#BK-305 Articulation Roundup • ©2003 Super Duper® Publications • www.superduperinc.com • 1-800-277-8737

www.superduperinc.com • 1-800-277-8737

#BK-305 Articulation Roundup • ©2003 Super Duper® Publications

homew̲ork

bow̲ing

tow̲er

bow-w̲ow

aw̲ake

tow̲el

show̲er

sidew̲alk

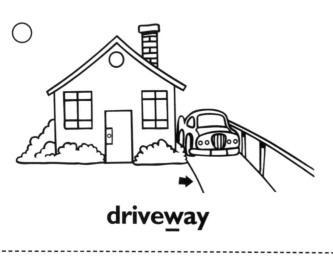

drive_w_ay

sand_w_ich

sea_w_eed

rew_w_ard

micro_w_ave

pocket _w_atch

a_w_ard

wishing _w_ell

#BK-305 *Articulation Roundup* • ©2003 Super Duper® Publications • www.superduperinc.com • 1-800-277-8737

#BK-305 Articulation Roundup · ©2003 Super Duper® Publications · www.superduperinc.com · 1-800-277-8737

rowing a boat

a sour lemon

a tall tower

a yummy sandwich

FLIGHT 332 BOARDING

going away

a wet towel

take a shower

blowing a whistle

The dog is in the sho_w_er.

The kitten naps on the to_w_el.

The woman is mo_w_ing the lawn.

The duck is on the side_w_alk.

He is blo_w_ing bubbles.

The kids eat sand_w_iches.

He is doing home_w_ork.

She builds a big to_w_er.

#BK-305 Articulation Roundup • ©2003 Super Duper® Publications • www.superduperinc.com • 1-800-277-8737

#BK-305 Articulation Roundup • ©2003 Super Duper® Publications • www.superduperinc.com • 1-800-277-8737

Initial Y

y̲ak

This Book Belongs to _____

Exercises to Promote the "Y" Sound

1. Find all the yellow things around the room. Have student practice a good "Y" sound.

2. To distinguish "W" from "Y," have the student smile while making the "Y" sound.

Word Discrimination

yawn   lawn

Help the student hear the difference between the "Y" and "L/W" sounds. Have the child point to each word as you say it.

Practice initial "Y" in syllables with long vowels.

yā (as in yale)
yē (as in yeast)
yī (as in yipes)
yō (as in yo-yo)
yū (as in youth)

Have the student say each syllable after you say it.

Practice initial "Y" in syllables with short vowels.

yă (as in yam)
yĕ (as in yell)
yĭ (as in yipee)
yŏ (as in yahoo)
yŭ (as in yucky)

Have the student say each syllable after you say it.

Sound Level

I'm practicing my final "Y" sound in:

___ syllables
___ words
___ phrases
___ sentences

Helper's Log

Sun.	Mon.	Tues.	Wed.	Thurs.	Fri.	Sat.

Please initial the days that you helped _____ say the final "Y" sound.

1A

y̲ell

2A

y̲oke

1B

w̲ell

2B

w̲oke

3A

y̲awn

4A

y̲am

3B

l̲awn

4B

l̲amb

#BK-305 Articulation Roundup · ©2003 Super Duper® Publications · www.superduperinc.com · 1-800-277-8737

#BK-305 Articulation Roundup • ©2003 Super Duper® Publications • www.superduperinc.com • 1-800-277-8737

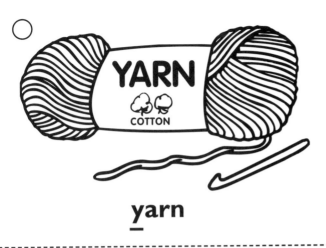

yarn

yell

you

yoke

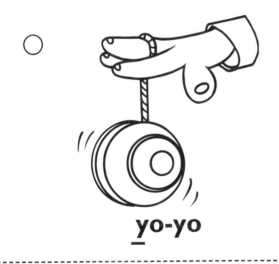

yo-yo

yummy

yawning

yucky

a <u>y</u>ummy cookie

a new <u>y</u>o-<u>y</u>o

#BK-305 Articulation Roundup • ©2003 Super Duper® Publications • www.superduperinc.com • 1-800-277-8737

a <u>y</u>ellow bus

<u>y</u>ell in the <u>y</u>ard

Do <u>y</u>ou have a <u>y</u>o-yo?

The <u>y</u>ak is in the <u>y</u>ard.

The <u>y</u>oung man rides a <u>u</u>nicycle.

The cowboy <u>y</u>ells, "<u>Y</u>ippee!"

#BK-305 Articulation Roundup • ©2003 Super Duper® Publications • www.superduperinc.com • 1-800-277-8737

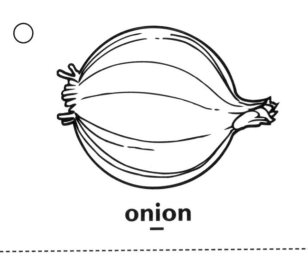

on_ion

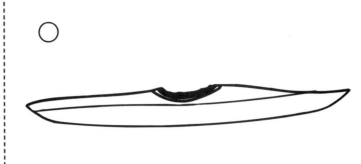

ka_yak

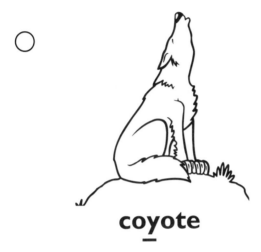

co_yote

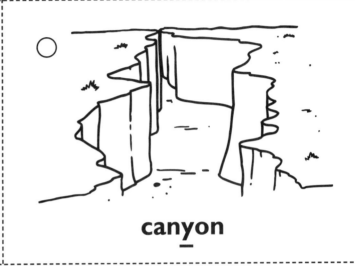

can_yon

dep_uty

COUNTY COURTHOUSE

law_yer

egg _yolk

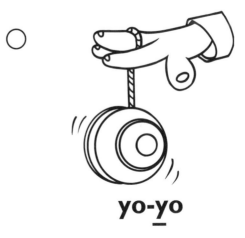

yo-_yo

New Year

Hawaiian

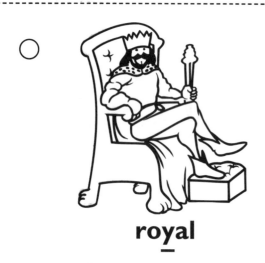

royal

ambulance

New York

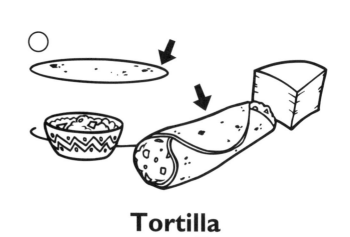

Tortilla

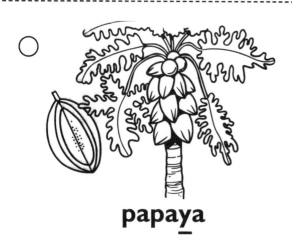

papaya

figure skate

Cut on dotted line

#BK-305 *Articulation Roundup* • ©2003 Super Duper® Publications • www.superduperinc.com • 1-800-277-8737

a young coyote

paddling a kayak

#BK-305 Articulation Roundup • ©2003 Super Duper® Publications • www.superduperinc.com • 1-800-277-8737

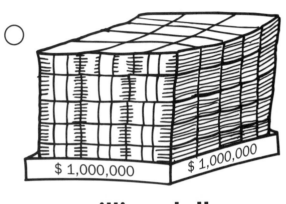

$ 1,000,000 $ 1,000,000

a million dollars

a deputy sheriff

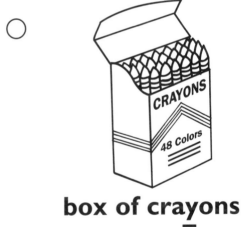

CRAYONS
48 Colors

box of crayons

onion soup

Happy New Year

in my backyard

The lawyer has a briefcase.

William lives in New York.

The royal family
lives in a castle.

She grows onions
in the backyard.

The coyote walks
in the canyon.

He buys an action figure.

The kid plays with a yo-yo.

The deputy is on a stallion.

RESOURCE SECTION

★ **Target Book Covers**

★ **Awards & Certificates**

★ **Additional Therapy Ideas**

#BK-305 *Articulation Roundup* • ©2003 Super Duper® Publications • www.superduperinc.com • 1-800-277-8737

#BK-305 Articulation Roundup • ©2003 Super Duper® Publications • www.superduperinc.com • 1-800-277-8737

#BK-305 Articulation Roundup · ©2003 Super Duper® Publications · www.superduperinc.com · 1-800-277-8737

Your Speech is
DINO-MITE!

Student

Date

Speech-Language Pathologist

#BK-305 Articulation Roundup • ©2003 Super Duper® Publications • www.superduperinc.com • 1-800-277-8737

READ ALL ABOUT IT!

_____ can produce the _____ sound in words.

Great speech is big news!

_____ Date

Speech-Language Pathologist

EXTRA! EXTRA! EXTRA!

#BK-305 Articulation Roundup • ©2003 Super Duper® Publications • www.superduperinc.com • 1-800-277-8737

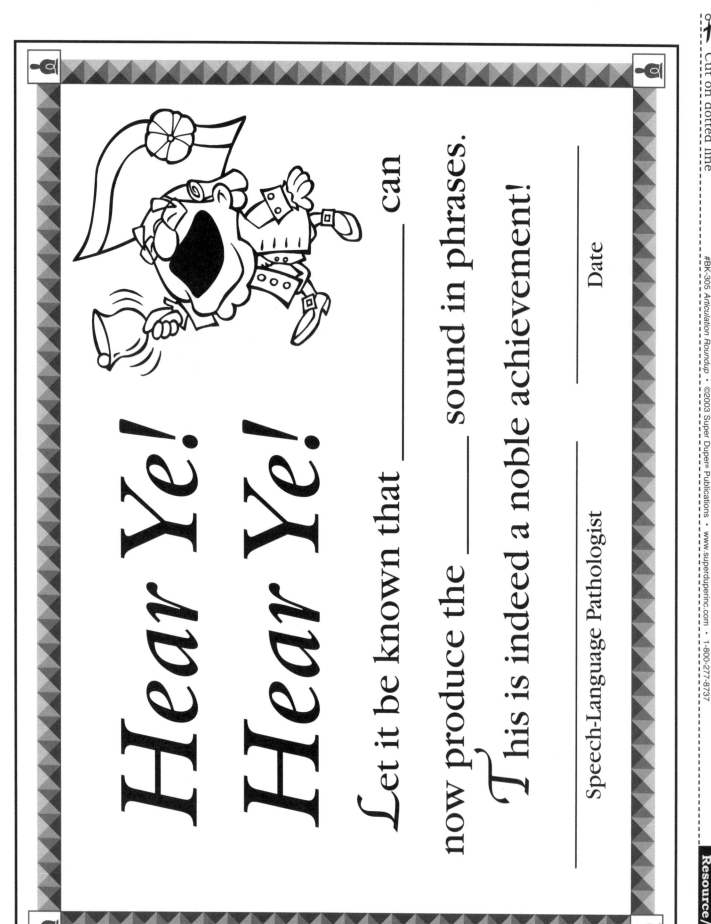

Hear Ye!
Hear Ye!

Let it be known that _____ can

now produce the _____ sound in phrases.

This is indeed a noble achievement!

_____
Date

Speech-Language Pathologist

#BK-305 Articulation Roundup • ©2003 Super Duper® Publications • www.superduperinc.com • 1-800-277-8737

Congratulations

can produce the

_____
Honored Student

_____
sound in sentences.

Just thought you should know.

Proudly presented by _____ on _____

_____   _____
SLP   Date

#BK-305 *Articulation Roundup* • ©2003 Super Duper® Publications • www.superduperinc.com • 1-800-277-8737

Up, Up, and Away

with

Outstanding

Speech

_____ can now produce
Student

the _____ sound in syllables.

Great job!

_____ Speech-Language Pathologist

_____ Date

#BK-305 Articulation Roundup • ©2003 Super Duper® Publications • www.superduperinc.com • 1-800-277-8737

#BK-305 *Articulation Roundup* • ©2003 Super Duper® Publications • www.superduperinc.com • 1-800-277-8737

Doggone Good Good Speech

_____'s speech has

really improved!

Keep up the doggone good work!

_____

Date

_____

Speech-Language Pathologist

Here's the Scoop!

_____ has
completed the speech
program at _____

Presented by _____
Speech-Language Pathologist

on _____

Cut on dotted line

#BK-305 Articulation Roundup · ©2003 Super Duper® Publications · www.superduperinc.com · 1-800-277-8737

Resource/Page 208

#BK-305 Articulation Roundup • ©2003 Super Duper® Publications • www.superduperinc.com • 1-800-277-8737

Speech Diploma

_____ has

successfully completed
the Speech Program

at _____.

Proudly presented by _____

_____ SLP
on _____. Congratulations!

SOUNDS LIKE YOUR _____ SOUND IS IMPROVING!

_____
Speech-Language Pathologist

_____
Date

#BK-305 Articulation Roundup • ©2003 Super Duper® Publications • www.superduperinc.com • 1-800-277-8737

#BK-305 Articulation Roundup • ©2003 Super Duper® Publications • www.superduperinc.com • 1-800-277-8737

Three Cheers for

_____ !

Your _____

Sound is Getting

Better!

_____

Speech-Language Pathologist

_____

Date

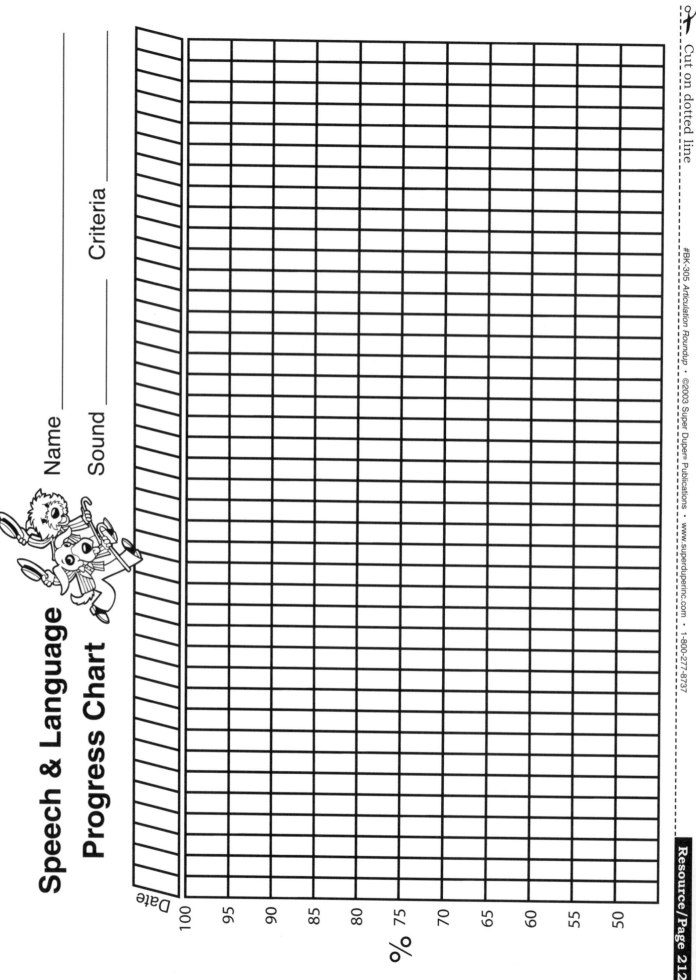

Speech & Language
Progress Chart

Name _____

Sound _____

Criteria _____

Date

% 100 95 90 85 80 75 70 65 60 55 50

#BK-305 Articulation Roundup · ©2003 Super Duper® Publications · www.superduperinc.com · 1-800-277-8737

Additional Ideas for Therapy

1. Treasure Hunt – The student tries to find hidden pictures or objects in the classroom. When the object/picture is found, the student names it or uses the word in a sentence.

2. Puzzle Mania – The student is given one piece of a puzzle for every correct response. Once the pieces have been collected, the student can put the puzzle together.

3. Buried Treasure – Pictures or objects are buried in a box of rice, sand, beans, etc. The student finds the target picture/object and then names it.

4. Jump Rope Frenzy – The student jumps rope while producing the target sound or word with every jump.

5. Fishing Game – Make a fishing pole using a small wooden dowel with a string attached. (The string should be approximately 16 to 18 inches.) Place a magnet at the end of the string. (The horseshoe shaped magnets work the best.) Attach a paper clip, to each target picture. Now the student can fish for the target words by dropping the magnet at the end of the fishing pole to "catch" a target picture.

6. Clothespin Drop – The student can kneel or stand on a chair and drop clothespins into a jar below. With each drop, the student will verbalize the target word.

7. Fruit Loop®/Cheerios® Paste-up – The student will glue Fruit Loops® or Cheerios® to a target word or sound on the tagboard.

8. Hopscotch – The clinician makes a hopscotch outline using chalk or masking tape. One target picture is placed on each square of the hopscotch outline. The student names the target picture prior to hopping to the next square.

9. Guessing Game – The clinician tapes a target word on the student's back. The student must guess the unknown picture by asking yes/no questions to the clinician or other students.

10. Hidden Pictures – Objects or target pictures are hidden around the room. The clinician turns off the lights and gives the student a flashlight to hunt for them. The student names each picture/object as it is found.

Cut on dotted line

#BK-305 Articulation Roundup • ©2003 Super Duper® Publications • www.superduperinc.com • 1-800-277-8737

11. Hot Potato – Two target pictures are taped to a beanbag hot potato or a real potato. As the potato is tossed, the student names the target picture.

12. Stopwatch Race – The student names as many target pictures as possible in one minute.

13. Play Dough Sculptures – The student reproduces the target pictures using play dough.

14. Building Blocks – The student receives one block for every correct response. He/she can build towers, houses, buildings, etc.

15. Bowling Bonanza – The clinician tapes target words on toy bowling pins. The student tries to knock down as many pins as he/she can with the bowling ball. The student then names all the target pictures on the pins that were knocked down.

16. Memory Game – The clinician chooses four or more target pictures. The student then looks at the picture for 30 seconds. The student is asked to close his/her eyes as the clinician turns one picture over. The student opens his/her eyes and has to guess which picture has been turned over.

17. Feely Box or Grab Bag – The clinician fills a box or bag with objects/pictures containing the target sounds. The student then pulls out each object/picture and names it.

18. Beanbag Toss – The student will throw a beanbag through a standing figure with holes in it. (The figure can be a clown, cowboy, etc.) Above each hole, a target picture can be taped. When the student throws a beanbag through a hole, he/she names the target picture.

19. Target Word Charades – The student acts out a target word such as "tree," "lamb," "snake," etc. Other students take turns guessing the target word.

20. Listen "Beary" Carefully – The student listens and corrects a word in a sentence. For example, with the "St-" sounds:

> The red light means to h-op. (stop)
> I like to sing "Twinkle, Twinkle, Little c-ar." (star)

#BK-305 Articulation Roundup • ©2003 Super Duper® Publications • www.superduperinc.com • 1-800-277-8737